HEAR

WHAT
THE SPIRIT
IS SAYING

A PRACTICAL APPROACH TO THE
SEVEN CHURCHES OF REVELATION

HEAR

WHAT

THE SPIRIT

IS SAYING

A PRACTICAL APPROACH TO THE
SEVEN CHURCHES OF REVELATION

Dr. RAUL A. RIES

LOGOS MEDIA GROUP
22324 Golden Springs Drive
Diamond Bar, CA 91765-2449

Hear What the Spirit Is Saying:
A Practical Approach to the Seven Churches of Revelation

Copyright © 1993 Dr. Raul A. Ries
Published by Logos Media Group
Diamond Bar, CA 91765-2449
All rights reserved.

Library of Congress Catalog Card Number: 93-78422
ISBN 0-9637117-0-9

Unless otherwise indicated, Scripture references in this book are taken from the New King James Version, Copyright © 1979, 1980, 1982 by Thomas Nelson, Inc., Publishers.

Cover Design: Alejandro Alonso

I want to thank my pastor, Chuck Smith, for all the years he has invested in my life, and for the solid teaching of God's Word he has given me. Through all my years of learning the Scriptures I have come not only to love the Word of God, but also to develop an ear to hear what it is saying to my own personal life. This has been a key lesson that I have witnessed in and learned from the life of Chuck Smith as he has been consistent in his example and in his teaching. He is truly a servant of the Lord Jesus Christ.

-Contents-

1 An Overview **11**

2 The Letter to the **19**
Church of Ephesus

3 The Letter to the **35**
Church of Smyrna

4 The Letter to the **51**
Church of Pergamos

5 The Letter to the **71**
Church of Thyatira

6 The Letter to the **85**
Church of Sardis

7 The Letter to the **107**
Church of Philadelphia

8 The Letter to the **129**
Church of Laodicea

9 How to Be Born Again **149**

ONE

AN OVERVIEW

(Revelation 1:3)

Blessed is he who reads and those who hear the words of this prophecy, and keep those things which are written in it; for the time is near.

-1-

Looking at the context of the letters to the seven churches in the book of Revelation, chapter one deals with the past, chapters two and three deal with the present, and chapters four through twenty-two deal with the future. Chapters two and three are especially important to us because these two chapters are the final scriptural writings that deal directly with the present church of Jesus Christ.

First Thessalonians 4:16-17 tells us that Jesus will descend from heaven with a shout, and the sound of a trumpet. All born-again Christians who are alive on earth at that time will meet in the clouds with Jesus to be with Him for all eternity: "For the Lord Himself will descend from heaven with a shout, with the voice of an archangel, and with the trumpet of God. And the dead in Christ will rise first. Then we who are alive and remain shall be caught up together with them in the clouds to meet the Lord in the air. And thus we shall always be with the Lord."

This event has come to be known as the *rapture* of the church. Some say that the idea of the rapture is man-made because the word *rapture* does not appear in the Bible. However, the phrase in the above Thessalonians passage, "caught up," is translated from the Greek word *harpazo*, which means "to be snatched up." The Latin Vulgate translation of the same word is *rapio*, from which we derive the term rapture.

Another phrase that needs defining is *the Great Tribulation.* The Great Tribulation refers to a precise seven-year period of unprecedented divine and supernatural judgment upon the world in which God again will deal exclusively with the Jews. The world ruler during this time of global tribulation is known in Scripture as the *Antichrist*, or *son of perdition.* The condition of the world during that period will be more awful than any other time in man's existence. The Bible tells us in several passages that this seven-year period will be divided into two equal portions of time. These portions are described as being 3-1/2 years, or 42 months, or 1,260 days (based on a lunar calendar of 360 days, rather than the modern 365.25 day solar calendar).

Daniel 9:27 says, "Then he [the Antichrist] shall confirm a covenant with many for one week; but in the middle of the week he shall bring an end to sacrifice and offering. And on the wing of abominations shall be one who makes desolate, even until the consummation, which is determined, is poured out on the desolate." (The meaning of the word *week* in the original Hebrew text is literally a "group of seven," and in this case, means seven years.)

Revelation 13:5, 7 describes the same period: "And he [the Antichrist] was given a mouth speaking great things and blasphemies, and he was given authority to continue for forty-two months . . . . It was granted to him to make war with the saints and to overcome them. And authority was given him over every tribe, tongue, and nation."

The first 3-1/2-year period will be the Antichrist's master deception of the entire world. This period will be a

time of global peace. During the following 3-1/2-year period, however, the Antichrist will execute everyone who
does not worship him as God. In addition, God will afflict
all of the people remaining on earth with increasingly hor-
rible plagues. These are described in chapter sixteen of
Revelation. All who take the mark of the Beast will sustain malignant sores all over their bodies, all living creatures in the sea will die, all rivers and springs will turn to
blood, there will be scorching heat from the sun, and finally, there will be darkness so oppressive that men will gnaw
their tongues to bloody pulp. In spite of this overwhelming
display of God's sovereignty, the people on earth will stubbornly refuse to acknowledge God as Lord.

There are three basic views concerning the rapture of
the church which have been debated by Bible scholars for
centuries: *pre-tribulation*, or that the church will be raptured *before* the tribulation begins, *mid-tribulation*, or that
the church will be raptured *at the 3-1/2-year mark,* or in the
middle of the tribulation, and *post-tribulation*, or that the
church will be raptured *after* the tribulation period has
ended. After studying the subject thoroughly and examin-
ing all the scriptural evidence concerning this exciting e-
vent in the church, it is my belief that the rapture will oc-
cur *before* the tribulation period begins.

An Overview of the Churches

The letters in chapters two and three of the book of
Revelation are not only written to seven actual churches in
Asia Minor during the time of John the Apostle's exile on
the island of Patmos, but they also describe seven distinct
periods of church history. The church of Ephesus repre-

sents the original, first century church, which began in
A.D. 30 and continued until about A.D. 99-100, at the
death of John.

The letter to the church of Smyrna describes the second period of church history, approximately A.D. 100-300.
The church of Smyrna is called the suffering church because more Christians died for their faith in Jesus Christ
during that period than during any other time. It was a
time of tremendous persecution by the Roman emperors.

The third period of church history is represented by
the church of Pergamos. Historically, this was the beginning of Emperor Constantine's pollution of the church with
all sorts of traditional rites. This was a state church, per-
meated with the pagan customs and practices of the world.
This church no longer cared about the things of God because it became a religion.

The church of Thyatira is historically the beginning of
the Roman Catholic Church. This system began around
A.D. 606, and continues through our present age, and will
continue through the Great Tribulation. It is considered to
be a church of idolatry.

The church of Sardis is the Protestant church, beginning with the Reformation in about 1520, and also continuing through the Great Tribulation. This church does not
seem to have the problem with idolatry that its predecessor
has, but nonetheless, it is called a dead church.

The sixth church is the church of Philadelphia. It is
the evangelistic church, beginning about 1750, and continuing only until the rapture. This church does not go into
the Great Tribulation, but will be taken out of the world at
the rapture. Jesus says that this church has little strength,
yet it keeps His Word and has not denied His name. This

church is truly looking for the return of Christ.

The last church is the church of Laodicea, beginning around 1900 with the introduction of neo-orthodoxy in which the concepts of biblical inspiration, illumination, and revelation were challenged, and then removed from seminary curriculums. This is the liberal church of today, rich and in need of nothing in their own eyes, and continues through the Tribulation period.

The important thing to remember as we study the letters to the seven churches is that there are elements of these churches in every Christian. We are not merely studying history, or reading someone else's mail; we clearly are called to examine our hearts to see if there are elements in our lives that displease Jesus Christ. If there are, we need to heed the corrections that Jesus gives to each one of the churches.

TWO

THE LETTER TO THE CHURCH OF EPHESUS

(Revelation 2:1-7)

"To the angel of the church of Ephesus write, 'These things says He who holds the seven stars in His right hand, who walks in the midst of the seven golden lampstands: "I know your works, your labor, your patience, and that you cannot bear those who are evil. And you have tested those who say they are apostles and are not, and have found them liars; and you have persevered and have patience, and have labored for My name's sake and have not become weary. Nevertheless I have this against you, that you have left your first love. Remember therefore from where you have fallen; repent and do the first works, or else I will come to you quickly and remove your lampstand from its place–unless you repent. But this you have, that you hate the deeds of the Nicolaitans, which I also hate. He who has an ear, let him hear what the Spirit says to the churches. To him who overcomes I will give to eat from the tree of life, which is in the midst of the Paradise of God." ' "

-2-

The message to the church of Ephesus is a very important message for the church today, because the church of Ephesus did not leave God for idols; they did not settle in the world; they did not become liberal in their theology; they did not quit doing the work of the Lord; they simply, but tragically, left their first love—Jesus Christ.

This is the loveless church. Its members work hard; they go out and witness; they study the Bible; they have regular prayer meetings; they have an abundance of church programs. Their problem, however, is that they do everything as works, rather than out of love. This is a very dangerous position to be in, because the works may seem as though they are being done for the Lord, when in actuality, they are being done simply to build personal treasures, or even out of habit. Our work for the Lord must be motivated always by our love for Him and His love for us.

The letter is addressed to **the angel of the church of Ephesus**. The Greek word for angel used here is *aggelos*, meaning "messenger," and also "pastor." This message is to the pastor of the church. The name Ephesus means "desirable ones."

From about A.D. 30 to A.D. 100, the church of Ephesus was the foremost of the Asian churches. The city of Ephesus was located on the eastern shoreline of what is now called the Aegean Sea, in the fertile, densely populated province of Lydia, about 150 miles directly east of Athens, Greece, and about 35 miles north of Miletus. It was situated at the mouth of the Custer River, at the junction of several trade routes, which made it a very prosperous city in the Roman-occupied territory of Asia Minor. Being a seaport, it was a strong commercial center, as well as a religious center, with both Jews and Gentiles worshipping there.

Ephesus was particularly noted for the temple of Diana (Roman name) or Artemis (Greek name), one of the seven wonders of the ancient world. Diana, the goddess of sex and fertility, was described as a woman with a thousand breasts. There were also one thousand prostitutes who served in Diana's temple. These prostitutes would go down into the city and seduce the people, the money earned going back into the temple for the priests and priestesses. It was a very lucrative religion. The city also gained a substantial revenue from the sale of amulets, or good luck charms. The society placed great importance on all sorts of superstitions, but their lives were completely empty of any true faith. Today, the ancient city of Ephesus is still populated, but it has deteriorated into a miserable, dying Turkish village, named Ayasaluk.

The book of Ephesians, as well as Acts 19-21, provide a good historical background for the Ephesian church. The Apostle Paul spent almost three years in Ephesus on his third missionary journey. He gave us the great sermon in Acts 20 when he spoke to the elders of the Ephesian church, warning them that when he would depart, various wolves would rise up from within the church to seduce the people.

In Acts 19, when Paul first came to Ephesus, he spoke to twelve men who had been disciples of Apollos. Since Apollos had been a follower of John the Baptist, he had only taught these men John's baptism of repentance from sin. Paul discovered that they had never heard of the Holy Spirit, so he explained to them the doctrine of the Holy Spirit. Upon laying hands on each one of them, they were all baptized in the Holy Spirit and spoke in tongues.

Now, just thirty short years later, John the Beloved, at about ninety-eight years old, writes this stern message from the resurrected Jesus Christ to the church of Ephesus. Christ's complaint is that the church has left its first love. After thirty years as a powerful witness for the Lord, the church of Ephesus is facing death. It has become a loveless church. The people did not *lose* their first love, they *left* their first love; they walked away from it.

Notice that the responsibility is upon the individual. Jesus did not leave them; they left Him. This is always the case. Jesus is faithful in His relationship to us; we are not always faithful in our relationship to Him. We, the church of Jesus Christ, must separate ourselves from the world, and ask God to minister to us individually, especially if we are in a backslidden condition. This letter describes a person who is backslidden.

Remembering Our First Love

Do you remember when you first came to Jesus Christ, and how excited you were? No one could keep you quiet about your Lord and Savior; you were on fire for Him. All you could talk about was what the Lord was doing in your life. You came to Bible studies every time the doors were

open. You felt a burden for your lost family and friends.
You tried to share the love of Jesus with them at every possible opportunity. You invited them to Bible studies when-
ever you could talk them into going. You made yourself
accountable to people, and to God, because the fire of His
love was burning in your heart.

Then slowly, the fervency faded to the point that you
came to Bible studies only when you felt like it. You
found yourself justifying your behavior; you found yourself compromising your beliefs. You no longer talked
about the Lord to anyone who would listen, but instead,
"waited on the leading of the Spirit." You now needed an
opening large enough to drive a truck through before you
would share the gospel of Christ with someone. Your
boldness had gone. The fire was no longer burning. You
were no longer in love with the Lord. You were backslidden.

God has given the church the institution of marriage as
a model of our relationship with Jesus. As the marriage
progresses, the love develops and matures. For the first six
months, or year, or two years, some more, some less, the
newly married couple sits together in church arm-in-arm.
The husband opens all of the doors for his wife; he sends
her flowers regularly; they leave little love notes for each
other; they call each other regularly when they are at work;
they can hardly stand to be apart. Their love is manifested
in many significant and pleasing outward gestures.

Then slowly, sometimes unnoticably at first, signs of
dissatisfaction begin to appear, little signs that the excitement is wearing off: no more hand-holding, or door-open-
ing, or notewriting, or phone calls, or flowers.

As a necessary precaution to this happening, the couple must continually rekindle that original flame of love. If they neglect it, then eventually their marriage will end in divorce.

This is to what Jesus is referring when He says that the church of Ephesus has left its first love. The believers in Ephesus have lost the excitement they had when they first established their relationship with Him. The same can happen in our relationship with Jesus Christ. If we neglect our love for Him, we will gradually drift away, until we are separated totally from Him, and miserable. Jesus is teaching us that we need to be careful how we treat our relationship with Him. We need to daily exercise our love for Him, just as we need to exercise our love for our spouses. We should be excited to read His Word and to pray to Him. We should look forward to our time of fellowship with Him.

Slip-Sliding Away

Revelation chapter one describes seven unique characteristics of Jesus Christ, and then in chapters two and three, we see one of those characteristics manifested in each of the seven churches.

In 2:1 we read, **He who holds the seven stars in His right hand, who walks in the midst of the seven golden lampstands . . . .** The position of Jesus Christ is in the midst of the churches, not outside, not behind, not out in front. Jesus should be in the center of our relationship with Him, just as the tabernacle was in the center of the Israelite camp in the Old Testament. Too often, churches are man-centered, not Christ-centered.

In verses two and three, Jesus proclaims, **I know your**

works, your labor, your patience, and that you cannot bear those who are evil. And you have tested those who say they are apostles and are not, and have found them liars; and you have persevered and have patience, and have labored for My name's sake and have not become weary. This church has spiritual discernment. It cannot bear people who are evil. Acts 20 describes how false teachers would rise up within the church at Ephesus after Paul left, and come against the leadership. Jesus tells the church that they have done well in guarding against this happening. Nevertheless, they have a major problem.

You can attend church your whole life, and go to all of the church functions and events, and yet, your relationship with Jesus Christ can be dead. The people whom Jesus describes here are not growing closer to Him, even though they are going through all the motions. Just as some people endure a bad marriage because they want to avoid a divorce, the church of Ephesus is enduring with Jesus, long after their love for Him has died. There is a clear and stern warning given, however: unless they repent and do their first works, Jesus will come quickly and remove His presence from them. The warning needs to be taken seriously by the modern church—where Christ is not wanted and sought after daily with a sincere and fervent heart, He will not remain.

A person can go through all the motions of being a Christian—studying, preaching, witnessing, going here and there for God, while the fire of love for Jesus has dwindled in his heart. A person can have discernment, works, patience, strenuous and exhausting labor for God, hate evil, and yet, be sliding away from God at the same time. This downslide often results in a severely judgmental attitude on the part of the person backsliding, forcing him further from the truth. The whole point is that we really need to examine our own lives to make sure that we understand what is going on inside our hearts.

Verse four introduces the terrifying revelation: **Nevertheless I have this against you, that you have left your first love.** Even though we are children of God, Jesus can have something against us. The two most important commandments that Jesus gave us in Matthew 22:37-40 are that we should love the Lord our God with all our hearts, with all our souls, and with all our minds, and that we should love our neighbor as ourselves. Jeremiah 2:1 gives us a beautiful illustration of this truth. God is speaking to the nation of Israel through the young prophet Jeremiah, just before judgment came to the southern kingdom:

> Moreover the word of the LORD came to me, saying, "Go and cry in the hearing of Jerusalem, saying, 'Thus says the LORD: "I remember you, the kindness of your youth, the love of your betrothal, when you went after Me in the wilderness, in a land that was not sown. Israel was holiness to the LORD, the firstfruits of His increase. All that devour him will offend; disaster will come upon them," says the LORD.' " Hear the word of the LORD, O house of Jacob and all the families of the house of Israel. Thus says the LORD: "What injustice have your fathers found in Me, that they have gone far from Me, have followed idols, and have become idolaters? Neither did they say, 'Where is the LORD, who brought us up out of the land of Egypt, who led us through the wilderness, through a land of deserts and pits, through a land of drought and the shadow of death, through a land that no one crossed and where no one dwelt?' I brought you into a bountiful country, to eat its fruit and its goodness. But when you

> entered, you defiled My land and made My heritage
> an abomination. The priests did not say, 'Where is
> the LORD?' And those who handle the law did not
> know Me; the rulers also transgressed against Me;
> the prophets prophesied by Baal, and walked after
> things that do not profit."

God's complaint against the nation of Israel is the same complaint of Jesus Christ against the church of Ephesus. The children of Israel were so in love with God when He first led them out of Egypt into the Promised Land, but then their love quickly grew cold. God asks them, "In what way have I offended you that you have gone after other gods?" Their love for the Lord had grown cold.

Hebrews 13:5 promises that God will never leave us or forsake us. We are the ones who leave Him for other things. The children of Israel left God for all kinds of foreign gods. Instead of worshiping God, they delved into astrology, burned their babies in the arms of the god Molech, and copied the customs of the nations around them, which God commanded them *not* to do. Rather than living separately from the surrounding heathen cultures, they imitated them, and became like them.

How many people have you known who had been on fire for the Lord at one time, and with whom you have enjoyed great times of fellowship, and who now have gone back into the world? You run into them now or then, or hear about them, and it seems as though their sin is worse than it was before they first came to the Lord. This is because of the knowledge and accountability of the Word of God which they had once possessed. In 2 Peter 2:22 Peter writes, "But it has happened to them according to the true proverb: 'A dog returns to his own vomit,' and, 'a sow, having washed, to her wallowing in the mire.' "

The problem with the church today is that we, too, copy everything from the world. We copy its music; we copy its styles. God has called us to be imitators of Him, not of man. He gives us the wisdom and knowledge to live our lives far above the ways of the heathen world. We must live in the world, but we certainly do not have to imitate the world. We are only strangers and pilgrims in this world. First John 2:15 tells us, "Do not love the world or the things in the world. If anyone loves the world, the love of the Father is not in him."

No one who has personally known Jesus Christ and experienced the forgiveness of sin, can ever go back into the world and be the same as he was before he came to Jesus. If we ever go back into our old lifestyle of sin, we will be completely miserable because of our personal knowledge of Christ. If we refuse to repent, and continue in our own stubborn ways, our hearts will gradually harden against the Lord, just as Romans chapter one says.

Keep in mind that the people to whom Jesus is talking in the letters to the seven churches are Christians. If you are in a position right now, where you are not as much in love with Jesus Christ as when you first came to Him, then you are already backsliding. If you are not growing more and more in love with Jesus Christ everyday, then you are backsliding. Unless you truly repent, it is only a matter of time until you will find yourself back in the world, as so many once sincere people have done. If your primary source of fellowship is with non-Christians, they will eventually bring you down. Sooner or later, you will compromise; you will give in to temptation.

The only way to keep yourself in the fervent love of Christ, as Jude says in verse twenty-one, is to daily keep yourself in prayer, the Word, and fellowship with godly believers who are mature and love the Lord. If you have to cut off relationships because they are dragging you away from the Lord, then cut them off. God will honor your decision to follow and obey Him.

If your marriage is not working, you need to repent, and come back to your first love. Husbands need to take the leadership of their homes. As they submit to God, they will begin to make godly decisions, and their wives will begin to submit to them. Instead of yelling and screaming, husbands should humble themselves before their wives, and get on their knees to God, *before* they get into the flesh.

The Way Back

Is there then a solution if we have left our first love? Yes. The Lord's correction comes in Revelation 2:5, **Remember therefore from where you have fallen; repent and do the first works, or else I will come to you quickly and remove your lampstand from its place–unless you repent.** In order to rekindle our flame of love for Jesus Christ, we must regain a proper perspective, and get our priorities in order. Only a godly sorrow will lead to true repentance. A lot of people repent with tears and sorrow, like Esau when he discovered that he had lost his birthright, or Saul when he played the role of a priest in disobedience to God, or Judas when he betrayed Jesus, but it is not godly sorrow; they are only sorry that they got caught, or that there are consequences to their sins. That is not repentance. Repentance is from the heart; it is true and agonizing sorrow for what has been done, like Peter had after denying his Lord three times. Repentance is turning away from sin.

How does a person prove his repentant heart? By not doing what he used to do; by living a new life in Christ Jesus. In 2 Corinthians 5:17 Paul writes, "Therefore, if anyone is in Christ, he is a new creation; old things have passed away; behold, all things have become new." The evidence that our sins are really forgiven by Christ is that the old things are gone, and we make sure that they remain gone by putting off the old man, and putting on the new man in Christ.

Nothing in the world can take the place of God in our lives: not our boyfriends or our girlfriends, not our husbands or our wives, not our jobs or our hobbies. Jesus Christ must be first in our lives. Verse five also states the sad consequence of failing to repent, **. . . or else I will come to you quickly and remove your lampstand from its place–unless you repent.** The warning is that unless we repent, Jesus Christ will remove His presence from us and go somewhere else.

If we do not want to be used by God, or if we refuse to obey the Lord, He will use someone else to accomplish His purposes. His work will be accomplished, with us or without us. Many churches have died over the centuries for that very reason—they refused to obey God. The buildings still stand as a monument to what once was, but today they are empty. *People* are the church of Jesus Christ, not buildings. You and I are the church of Jesus Christ, and we need to heed the Spirit of God.

Encouragement comes in verse six, **But this you**

have, that you hate the deeds of the Nicolaitans, which I also hate. The word *nico* means "priest," and the word *laos* means "laity." The deeds of the Nicolaitans, then, was the lording, or ruling, of the priests over the people. Instead of each individual coming directly to God, as God had intended, the priests set up a system in which the people had to come through the priests in order to get to God. By the time the Roman Catholic Church had developed, this tradition was deeply embedded. First Timothy 2:5 says, "For there is one God and one Mediator between God and men, the Man Christ Jesus." Jesus Christ is our *only* high priest, and He is the *only* intercessor we need to the Father (Hebrews 7). Since Jesus Christ hated the doctrine of the Nicolaitans, we must hate it as well.

The familiar charge that is repeated in all seven letters to the churches is, **He who has an ear, let him hear what the Spirit says to the churches. To him who overcomes I will give to eat from the tree of life, which is in the midst of the Paradise of God.** Genesis 3 records the presence of the tree of life in the Garden of Eden. The tree of life mentioned in Revelation is in reference to the cross of Jesus Christ. Jesus Christ will be "in the midst of the Paradise of God," so He must be in the center of our lives.

In this life we have to make the choice whether we want to walk in the flesh or in the spirit. If we want to be overcomers, we must make the choice that Jesus gives us. In Matthew 16:24-25, Jesus tells us that the only choice which will lead to eternal life is self-denial: "Then Jesus said to His disciples, 'If anyone desires to come after Me, let him deny himself, and take up his cross, and follow Me. For whoever desires to save his life will lose it, and whoever loses his life for My sake will find it.' " Then in verse twenty-six, He asks the question, "For what is a man profited if he gains the whole world, and loses his own soul? Or what will a man give in exchange for his soul?" Are you willing to give up your eternal soul for temporary pleasure?

If you want to be an overcomer, you will take up the cross of Jesus Christ, which is the instrument of death, and you will follow after Jesus instead of after your own desires. When you do that, then you will begin to walk in the Spirit. And if you walk in the Spirit, you will have love, joy, peace, longsuffering, kindness, goodness, faithfulness, gentleness, and self-control, which are the fruits of the Spirit (Galatians 5:22-23). Then you will know that you are a child of God!

THREE

THE LETTER TO THE CHURCH OF SMYRNA

(Revelation 2:8-11)

"And to the angel of the church in Smyrna write, 'These things says the First and the Last, who was dead, and came to life: "I know your works, tribulation, and poverty (but you are rich); and I know the blasphemy of those who say they are Jews and are not, but are a synagogue of Satan. Do not fear any of those things which you are about to suffer. Indeed, the devil is about to throw some of you into prison, that you may be tested, and you will have tribulation ten days. Be faithful until death, and I will give you the crown of life. He who has an ear, let him hear what the Spirit says to the churches. He who overcomes shall not be hurt by the second death." ' "

-3-

The ancient city of Smyrna had a thriving Jewish community, and a sizable community of Jewish Christians. Smyrna was founded about three centuries before Christ by Alexander the Great. Due to the fact that it was on a direct trade route from India to Persia to Rome, it was a major commercial center in Asia Minor. Needless to say, Smyrna was a very wealthy city with a large upper-class population. Today, the city of Smyrna is called Izmir, and it is the capital city of the province of Lydia, with a population of about 250,000 people

Despite its affluent setting, the church of Smyrna became known as "the martyr church," or "the persecuted church." Along with the church of Philadelphia, it is the only other church that receives no condemnation from Jesus in His seven messages to the churches. Historically, the church of Smyrna was established about A.D. 100 and continued until about A.D. 312. Out of all the churches, Smyrna suffered extremely severe persecution. Church historian Tertullian (c. A.D. 160-230) said that the blood of the martyrs is the seed of the church. This statement was certainly true of the church of Smyrna.

The name Smyrna means "bitterness," from the root word *myrrh*. Myrrh was a bitter tasting gum resin that was taken from a shrub which grows in the western part of Asia

Minor. The Scriptures record three uses for it: as an ingredient in making perfumes (Psalm 45:8), as one of the ingredients of holy anointing oil for the priests (Exodus 30:23), and as an embalming fluid for dead bodies (John 19:39).

The assembly at Smyrna was severely persecuted for their faith in Jesus Christ. In order to understand the difficulty that they experienced in maintaining their commitment to Jesus Christ, it is important to understand the culture and type of government that was in power at the time. The Roman Empire ruled the entire known world, and its domination was especially pronounced in the regions of Asia Minor. The reigning Roman emperor, Caesar Nero, was referred to as the Beast, because he brought great persecution to the early church. For instance, in the evenings, as he sat on his balcony playing one of his stringed instruments, he would have Christians tied to poles in his courtyard, tarred, and lit on fire to illuminate his gardens. He not only had an intense hatred for Christians, but the evidence of his actions demonstrated that he was a deeply psychotic individual.

History records that the Apostle Paul met with Nero twice. Their first meeting produced nothing of note. On the second occasion, however, it is reported that because of his rejection of the truth from Paul, Nero became demon-possessed. Eventually, he set the entire city of Rome ablaze, then blamed it on the Christians. The burning of Rome by Nero was the beginning of severe Christian persecution throughout the Roman Empire. Women, children, parents, and grandparents were tortured and slaughtered. Some of them were cut in half; some were thrown into lions' dens; some were killed by gladiators; some were ripped apart by horses.

True Commitment

When people appeared before Nero, they were required to kneel, bow, and confess, "Caesar is Lord." If
they refused, they were tortured and killed. The moment a
person became a Christian in Smyrna, he lost his job, was
stripped of all of his wealth, and was considered dead by
his family. In modern terms he would have become a
street person. Imagine the great temptation in those days
not to become a Christian! There were very few insincere
Christians during that time because a person could lose his
life for committing himself to Christ.

There was not much sin in the church of Smyrna,
however, since the believers spent most of their time on
their knees asking God to help them through their present
trials and tribulations. They learned quickly that sin separated them from their Lord and Savior, and they could not
afford to neglect or ignore precious time of fellowship with
Him.

The Christians during that time period had a secret
code of identifying one another, which has become one of
the most well-known symbols of Christianity today,
although not many know its history. One person made an
arc in the sand with his foot. If the other person also was a
Christian, he, too, would trace an arc in the sand with his
foot that would connect at one end of the one already
drawn, and intersect at the other end, thus, forming a fish.

Eventually, though, the Roman soldiers discovered
this technique, and many Christians were killed as a result.
They then began to use letters of the Greek alphabet,

IGHTHUS, which stood for "Jesus Christ, God's Son, Savior." The Roman soldiers could not write the statement without themselves being guilty of high treason against Rome.

When Nero persecuted the Christians, about six million died for their faith in Jesus Christ. Joseph Stalin and Adolph Hitler committed similarly heinous crimes against mankind in this century in the Soviet Union and Europe. Although a daily lifestyle under severe persecution is almost inconceivable for us today in the United States, nonetheless, more than 1.5 million babies every year are tortured and murdered in the abortion process (more than 25 million since 1972). Is persecution of the Christian church in America around the corner?

In the catacombs in Rome, early Christian writings are visible on the walls. The Christians were forced to hide like animals. Betrayal by friends and enemies was common. Commitments to Christ were sincere. The stakes were high—deny Christ, or be killed. A person obeyed God, or obeyed man. That is why Christ's message to the church of Smyrna basically says, "Hang in there. Be faithful until death, and I will give you the crown of life."

The Wicked Emperors

The following is a brief list of the ten Roman emperors who ruled during the Roman Empire's great persecution of the Christian church:

1. Nero (A.D. 54-68). He beheaded the Apostle Paul and crucified the Apostle Peter upside-down. The fourth chapter of 2 Timothy contains Paul's final

writings before he was killed, in which he summarizes his entire life, "For I am already being poured
out as a drink offering, and the time of my depar-
ture is at hand. I have fought the good fight, I have
finished the race, I have kept the faith. Finally,
there is laid up for me the crown of righteousness,
which the Lord, the righteous Judge, will give to
me on that Day." Historians tell us that because of
Paul's testimony, the Roman centurions who took
him bound in chains into the arena to be beheaded,
cried out saying, "Caesar, I, too, am now a Christian!" Consequently, they, too, were martyred for
Jesus Christ. Paul mentions several places in his
letters that he was able to win many of the house-
hold of Caesar to the Lord. The Apostle Paul was a
man who recognized God's purpose in everything
that happened to him. He viewed his chains merely
as a measure to prevent the guards from escaping
the Gospel of Jesus Christ.

Peter, on the other hand, started out weak, but then
finished strong. His second epistle reveals the
tremendous maturation that took place in Peter's
life during the course of his ministry. The Lord
Jesus, many years earlier, had prophesied that Peter
would die by crucifixion (John 21:18-19).
Tradition tells us that as Peter stood in front of
Nero, he said, "I am not worthy to be put to death
in the same manner as my Lord Jesus Christ.
Crucify me upside-down." Can you imagine the
torture that he went through being crucified
upside-down, his blood rushing painfully to his

head? It must have been a slow, agonizing death, and yet Peter died for Jesus Christ. So Nero killed two great Apostles.

2. Domitian (A.D. 90-96). He exiled the Apostle John to the island of Patmos after trying unsuccessfully to kill him by boiling him in oil. On Patmos, however, is where the Lord gave him the book of Revelation. John is the only Apostle who died a natural death. The rest of the Apostles, except for Judas, who committed suicide, all died by persecution.

3. Trajan (A.D. 98-117). He burned Ignatius at the stake.

4. Hadrian (A.D. 117-138). He killed Telesphorus.

5. Marcus Aurelius (A.D. 161-180). He killed Justin Martyr.

6. Septimus Severus (A.D. 202-211). He killed Irenaeus.

7. Maximinus (A.D. 235-236). He killed Ursula and Hippolytus.

8. Decius (A.D. 249-251). He began first empire-wide persecution, and killed Alexander of Jerusalem.

9. Valerian (A.D. 257-260). He killed Origen.

10. Diocletian (A.D. 303-311). He was one of the worst of the Roman emperors in terms of persecuion of Christians. Churches were destroyed. The Scriptures were burned. Sacrifices to gods were required by everyone.

With Jesus, No Fear in Death

Jesus represents Himself to the church of Smyrna as **the First and the Last, the Alpha and the Omega, the beginning and the end; the one who was dead, and has come to life.** In this representation we see the power of the resurrection. Jesus Christ was not just a good teacher, or merely a prophet from God, but He is the *living* God. Notice that He represents Himself to the church as the resurrected, powerful God. Only as such, could He promise eternal life to those who were faithful until death. Paul's sentiment of Philippians 1:21 captures this hope, "For to me, to live is Christ, and to die is gain." How can Paul say that to die is gain? Because he knew that the moment he died, he would immediately be in the presence of God. Have you ever thought about that? Many people have had the experience of being prepared for surgery in which the surgeons use a general anesthetic. The anesthesiologist instructs you to count backwards from ten, and you barely make it to eight before you are unconscious. The next thing you know, you are in the recovery room. Imagine what it must be like when you close your eyes, take your last breath, slip away into eternity, and then suddenly awake in the presence of God. The Lord encourages us in Psalm 116:15, "Precious in the sight of the LORD is the death of His saints." That gives us hope.

If you are a Christian, death is not suffering; it is victory. As a Christian, God's grace is upon your life at the moment of death, even violent death. If the Lord wants you to be a martyr, He will give you the strength to endure it when the time comes. You will not have to worry about the pain, because you will be so conscious of Him, that your eyes will not be on yourself, they will be on Jesus.

Acts 7 records the stoning death of Stephen, the first Christian martyr. As the angry Jewish Council smashed him with huge rocks, Stephen called on Jesus to receive his spirit and to forgive his murderers. It seems unlikely that he even felt any pain. He was only aware of Jesus. That is where our eyes always need to be—in life and in death—upon Jesus Christ, and not upon our circumstances.

The Christian Life is Hard

In verse nine, Jesus says, **I know your works, tribulation, and poverty (but you are rich) . . . .** He is not referring to financial wealth, but to spiritual riches. As Christians we are rich through the things of the Spirit. The word *tribulation* used in this verse literally means "to be under great pressure; under persecution." The word *poverty* refers to losing a job, a home, a family, or everything material in this world. When you decide to follow Jesus Christ, you must be willing to give up everything. Your family and friends may completely reject you. You may be called to the life of a martyr. Oftentimes, that was the life of the Christian in Smyrna. The martyr does not feel sorry for himself, but he stands upon the promises of Jesus Christ, and endures the persecution, because he believes in his God. Jesus Christ promised us, "I am with you always, even to the end of the age" (Matthew 28:20), and "I will never leave you nor forsake you" (Hebrews 13:5).

Following Christ, Not the Law

The second part of verse nine gives insight into the serious nature of the problem in Smyrna, **. . . and I know the blasphemy of those who say they are Jews and are not, but are a synagogue of Satan.** That is to say that there were Jews (Judaizers) who were trying to encourage the Jewish Christians to return to the Old Testament sacrificial system. They were trying to replace the work of God's grace with the works of the Law. These cynics of the Gospel of Jesus Christ were trying to put their own man-made traditions in place of a relationship with Jesus Christ. These people were disguising themselves as Jewish Christians until the persecution came, and then their true natures were revealed. They were phonies in the body of Christ. It is easy to speak the Christian language, and act like a Christian, that is, until persecution comes. Persecution has an inherently important purifying factor that separates the wheat from the tares, the sheep from the goats, the gold from the dross.

We all need to be very careful in our zealousness to serve God, that we do not slip into a works-based religion. We need to be careful with whom we bond. Make sure that your closest friends are spiritual people, not carnal. They must be people who are willing to pray with you and for you. They must be like-minded with you, and they must love Jesus Christ more than anyone else in the world. If Jesus Christ is number one in our lives, and our closest friends have that same priority, then all of the other issues in our lives will be simplified. Our eyes are on Jesus Christ, regardless of what anyone else is doing. We are to follow Jesus Christ rather than any man.

Be unique in your relationship with God. If other people want to do their thing, let them do their thing. Be secure in your relationship with Jesus Christ, because He is your Rock. Do not compromise, or justify your position. Make a stand for Jesus Christ, and nothing will move you. Many people want to see how close they can get to the edge, and still be a follower of Jesus Christ. They are foolish. Stay away from the edge; do not flirt with eternity. Concentrate on getting closer to Jesus, not to the edge.

No Fear in Christ

In verse ten, Jesus says, **Do not fear any of those things which you are about to suffer.** God is not the author of fear. God is love, and perfect love casts out all fear. If you really love Jesus Christ, and your relationship with Him is the first priority in your life, then who is there to fear? Paul the Apostle wrote to young Timothy that Christians have not been given the spirit of fear, but of power, love, and a sound mind. In Romans 8:35, 38, 39, he wrote, "Who shall separate us from the love of Christ? Shall tribulation, or distress, or persecution, or famine, or nakedness, or peril, or sword? . . . For I am persuaded that neither death nor life, nor angels nor principalities nor powers, nor things present nor things to come, nor height nor depth, nor any other created thing, shall be able to separate us from the love of God which is in Christ Jesus our Lord." Nothing can separate me from the love of Jesus Christ. He is my Lord and my God.

Satan the Liar

Revelation 2:10 says, **Indeed, the devil is about to throw some of you into prison, that you may be tested ....** Who is our adversary? Satan. He wants to throw some of us into prison because he hates us. He is not our friend! He does not even like us. Satan hates all of mankind with a hate so profound, we cannot even fully comprehend it. The irony of the life we live here on earth is that so often, even as Christians, we believe Satan as if he was our friend. He tells people, "If you follow me, I will make you famous." They answer, "What do I have to do?" "Just sign here on the dotted line, and give me your heart," he replies. Sadly, too many people fall for his lies.

Satan's ways may be fun for a while, but sooner or later he will be back to collect on the promises you made to him. Then, once you have given your life over to him, he will destroy you. His only objective is to destroy you. Each day that you say no to Christ, you say yes to Satan.

The reason we go through illnesses, and seemingly bad situations, is because God is putting us through the fire to prove our faith. Our tribulations are not because God dislikes us, or because He is sadistic, but because He is molding us toward an end result that only He knows. Although the process is sometimes quite painful, He is proving our faith in Him because He loves us. Take a look at the book of Job. Job was stripped of everything except life itself, and yet he was able to say in Job 1:21, "The LORD gave, and the LORD has taken away; blessed be the name of the LORD."

Final Victory in Christ

. . . And you will have tribulation ten days is symbolic of the ten Roman emperors who would persecute the Christian church. **Be faithful until death, and I will give you the crown of life.** There is a crown for those who are martyrs for Jesus Christ. They will be given the crown of life to wear for eternity. What a blessed thing that the Lord will give to us if we just put our trust in Him!

Finally, in verse eleven, Jesus again reminds readers to understand, **He who has an ear, let him hear what the Spirit says to the churches.** Make sure that *you* qualify to hear: **He who overcomes shall not be hurt by the second death.** What is the second death? The Lake of Fire. Jesus promises that if you live your life for Him now, you will never see the second death. He will keep you from the Lake of Fire, and He will give you the crown of life. Why has He given us this incredible promise? Because He loves us. Are you ready for the challenge to overcome sin and evil by the power and blood of Jesus Christ?

FOUR

THE LETTER TO THE CHURCH OF PERGAMOS

(Revelation 2:12-17)

"And to the angel of the church in Pergamos write, 'These things says He who has the sharp two-edged sword: I know your works, and where you dwell, where Satan's throne is. And you hold fast to My name, and did not deny My faith even in the days in which Antipas was My faithful martyr, who was killed among you, where Satan dwells. But I have a few things against you, because you have there those who hold the doctrine of Balaam, who taught Balak to put a stumbling block before the children of Israel, to eat things sacrificed to idols, and to commit sexual immorality. Thus you also have those who hold the doctrine of the Nicolaitans, which thing I hate. Repent, or else I will come to you quickly and will fight against them with the sword of My mouth. He who has an ear, let him hear what the Spirit says to the churches. To him who overcomes I will give some of the hidden manna to eat. And I will give him a white stone, and on the stone a new name written which no one knows except him who receives it.' "

-4-

The church of Pergamos is the beginning of the state church, based on the decree of the Roman emperor Constantine. This church now had the political clout of the Roman Empire behind it, but spiritually, it had become known as the "compromising church," or the "indulgent church." The Greek word *Pergamos* means "marriage or elevation," which indicates that this church was married to the world. In Revelation 2:9, Jesus says to the church of Smyrna, "I know your works, tribulation, and poverty (but you are rich); and I know the blasphemy of those who say they are Jews and are not, but are a synagogue of Satan." In Smyrna, Satan was outside of the church persecuting the true disciples of Jesus Christ. In the letter to the church of Pergamos, we see that Satan is no longer outside of the church, but he has joined the church. He is living right in the middle of the church. Satan realized that outward persecution was making the church stronger, so he changed his tactics, and joined the church. He tried to deteriorate the church of Jesus Christ from within.

The church of Pergamos began about A.D. 312 and continued until about A.D. 606. This was a church infected by idolatry. The occult traditions of ancient Babylon infiltrated the church. This letter was addressed to Christians who were drifting into worldliness and carnality, drifting away from a life governed by the Spirit, and into a life governed by the flesh. These people were straddling the fence, indulging in the appetites of the flesh: sexual immorality, idolatry, witchcraft, and selfish ambition. They were having trouble deciding which way to go.

Keep in mind as we study these churches, that they were not only seven actual churches in Asia Minor during the first century, but they also are indicative of seven periods of church history, and perhaps most importantly, the elements of these churches are prevalent in our churches today. You will find that you belong to at least one of these churches. If we really examine our lives, every one of us will find a little bit of ourselves in the church of Pergamos.

The biblical character who probably best represents the Pergamos church is Abraham's nephew, Lot. Remember that Lot's and Abraham's shepherds were having problems with each other, so Abraham proposed to Lot that they go separate ways. Abraham generously gave Lot the choice of land that he wanted. Lot looked toward Sodom and Gomorrah, and he saw that the land was green and very beautiful. This was Lot's first step toward backsliding. He did not look at the land with any spiritual discernment; he looked with indulging eyes. All he saw was the lush beauty of the fields and trees. He was not thinking of Abraham, but only of himself. The account in Genesis goes on to tell us that when he separated from Abraham, he did not go *into* the cities of Sodom and Gomorrah, but he set up his tent a safe distance from them. This was his second step toward backsliding, until, finally, he was sitting as a judge at the city gates.

A Backslidden State

These are the very same steps that Christians take when we slide away from God. First, we see the things of the world, and they look pleasant, so we move a little closer to them to get a better look, and before we know it, the attraction has drawn us to where we never thought we would have gone. Eventually, we actually become part of the world. We can see people at all three stages in the church today. Some are watching the world at a distance, some have begun to inch closer to the world, just to get a better look, and some have completely left their relationship with Jesus Christ, and have moved back into the world. There is much to be learned from Lot, because we all have the capacity to backslide.

If you have accepted Jesus Christ as your personal Lord and Savior, and you think that you can go back into the world to do what you did before you knew Christ, you will be the most miserable person in the entire universe. Once you have seen the light of Jesus Christ, and you have tasted of the grace and the goodness of God, you will never be the same. The person in a backslidden state is obviously miserable, but he deludes himself into believing that he is doing well. The problem is, that although he might be doing well physically, materialistically, and even emotionally for a while, he is spiritually bankrupt. He has no fellowship with God; his heart is gradually hardening against God. He begins to do things that he never used to do, even before he came to Christ. Because he has been deceived and because of the hardness of his heart, he no longer relies on God's Word for guidance; he no longer listens to God; he no longer talks to God. He is alone. He has discarded his spiritual protection, and he eventually finds himself in a completely miserable state.

A Brief History

Pergamos was a very wealthy city. The people made a lot of money, and they had become self-centered. The city was strong and impregnable, situated on the north bank of the Caucaus River. It was known as a city of kings as early as 241 B.C. Later, it became a Roman city. Today, there are about 14,000 people living there.

The people of Pergamos were greatly obsessed by the pursuit of knowledge and wisdom through reading, and had a library that boasted of more than 200,000 books. A Roman author by the name of Baro reported that it was Emenies II of Pergamos who restored the use of parchment for writing when the king of Egypt forbade the export of papyrus. Instead of using papyrus, however, which came exclusively from the banks of the Nile River, Emenies discovered that a similar end-product could be manufactured using wood pulp. The city of Pergamos became very rich from the invention of paper.

Pergamos was called the Royal City. There was an eight hundred-foot mountain in the city, on top of which was a statue of the Greek god Zeus. All of the Greek gods were worshipped there: Zeus, Athena, Dionysus, and Asclepius, and a whole long list of pagan gods.

Religion, Not Relationship

The brand of religion that came to be labeled as Christianity in Pergamos had its roots in the occult traditions of ancient Babylon. Both Roman and church history tell us that Constantine, who previously had been intrigued by Christianity, allegedly saw a vision of a fiery cross in the sky, and heard a voice saying, "In this sign, conquer," as he was preparing to go to battle. By A.D. 312, Constantine had become so affected by the idea of Christianity, that he made it the state religion. Everyone in the Roman empire became a Christian by decree of the emperor. Obviously, that did not mean that everyone under Roman domination suddenly turned to Jesus Christ as Lord and Savior, and embraced the teachings of the Bible. The decree simply re-labeled any existing religious practice as "Christianity," whether or not it had anything to do with the Gospel of Jesus Christ. From A.D. 312 on, then, the church became more Roman and less Christian in practice. The true Christians, however, recognized what was happening, and began separating themselves from the official state religion. As they separated themselves, though, they began to be persecuted again. The church became polluted because of all the things that were imported from Romanism.

Many rituals were developed in the church of Pergamos which bore strong resemblance to the ancient Babylonian forms of worship. For example, the Cheldon Tau, which was the elevation of a large T on the end of a pole, was eventually adopted by the church as the sign of the cross. Another development from ancient Babylon which made its way into the church was the rosary. There is also no scriptural basis for the celibacy of priests and nuns, but its counterpart comes from the pagan vestal virgins in Baby-lon. Other practices originating in the church of Pergamos which have become doctrines in the Roman Catholic church are:

-Praying for the dead (A.D. 300)
-The sign of the cross (A.D. 375)
-Worship of saints and angels (A.D. 394)
-The Roman Catholic Mass (A.D. 431)
-Worship of Mary (A.D. 500)
-Priests wearing robes and collars to separate them-
    selves from the laity (A.D. 593)
-Purgatory (A.D. 600).

Worship services began to be conducted in Latin, a language that only the priests understood. They ceased the practice of praying directly to Jesus, and replaced it with praying to Mary as intercessor. From this partial list, we can see how so many of the rituals that we have always considered to be Christian, are purely man-made, or worse, came from occult traditions. This is not Protestant propaganda designed to make the Roman Catholic Church look bad; these are historical, verifiable facts.

Religion was invented by man, not by God. Whether you are referring to Roman Catholicism, Protestantism, Jehovah's Witness, Mormonism, Krishna, Islam, Buddhism, Hinduism, or any other religion in the world, they are all man-made religions, or man trying to earn his way to God. True Christianity, on the other hand, is God making the way to Himself known to man.

The Truth of God's Word

What distinguishes Christianity from any other religion in the world is the relationship that Christians have with the true and living God through His Son Jesus Christ. Christianity is indeed a narrow-minded belief system. In order for a person to claim to be a Christian, there are certain precepts that necessarily must follow:

> The Bible is the only inspired, infallible, authoritative, inerrant Word of God (2 Timothy 3:16-17; 2 Peter 1:19-21). The Bible is the basis for all Christian doctrine, and no Christian doctrine comes from any other source but the Bible (Revelation 22:18-19). There is one God, eternally existent in three persons: Father, Son, and Holy Spirit (Genesis 1:1; Deuteronomy 6:4; Matthew 28:19; John 10:30). Jesus Christ is the only begotten Son of God (John 3:16), who came to earth born of a virgin (Isaiah 7:14; Matthew 1:23; Luke 1:34-35), was crucified (Matthew 27:35), died for the sins of all mankind (1 Corinthians 15:3; Ephesians 1:7; Hebrews 2:9), and resurrected from the dead in bodily form on the third day (John 11:25; Luke 24:39; 1 Corinthians 15:4). After appearing to over five hundred of His followers (1 Corinthians 15:6), He ascended to the right hand of God the Father (Mark 16:19). Someday, He will return to earth to judge all of mankind (Acts 1:11; Revelation 19:11-16). Those who have accepted Him as their personal Lord and Savior, will reign with Him forever (Matthew 19:28; Revelation 2:26). Those who have refused to follow Him will be cast into the Lake of Fire, where they will be tormented forever (Mark 9:43; Revelation 20:15). Jesus Christ is fully man (1 John 4:1-3; 1 Timothy 2:5), and fully God (John 8:58), being the second member of the Triune God.

The Work of the Holy Spirit

Jesus boldly states that Satan dwells right within the church of Pergamos. Satan has made the church of Pergamos his home. Despite this fact, though, there are people in the church who have remained pure before God. They have separated themselves from heathen idolatry, and they have made themselves witnesses of the true Gospel of Jesus Christ.

We must be careful as we share our faith in Jesus Christ that we don't try to convert people. That is the work of the Holy Spirit. Everyone must make a personal choice in this life. If you want to be a humanist, go for it. If you want to be an agnostic, be an agnostic. If you want to be religious, you are welcome to it. In the same way that Joshua made his open proclamation to the nation of Israel, however, I declare that as for me and my house, we will serve the Lord. We are going to be Christians!

Jesus teaches us in John 16:8, "And when He [the Holy Spirit] has come, He will convict the world of sin, and of righteousness, and of judgment." The Holy Spirit shows us righteousness and warns us of judgment. If you are trying to convince your mom or dad, or your brothers or sisters, or your friends, or your teachers, or your work associates, or anyone else, to accept Jesus Christ as Lord and Savior, you are going to be a very frustrated person. God never called us to convert people. He called us to share the Gospel, most importantly, by *living* the life of a Christian. He called us to trust in Him, to read His Word, to study, to pray, to fellowship, to get to know Him personally. As our lives are slowly conformed to the Spirit of Christ Jesus, then our living testimonies will affect others around us. They, in time, will come to know the knowledge of the truth according to God's perfect timing.

Many people seem to have no capacity to understand the truth. When you talk about Christ, they begin to get defensive. They accuse us of maintaining a narrow-minded opinion, or of judging them. The Bible is not our opinions; it is God's Word. Our opinions are inconsequential. We do not stand with Socrates, or Plato, or any of the secular philosophers. We do not stand with Buddha, or Krishna, or any of the world religions. We stand upon God's Word. If someone wants to argue with me about religion, he will have to argue based on the Word of God, because it is the only source of uncompromising truth on which we can depend. All I know is Jesus Christ, and Him crucified.

A Lesson About Compromise

The primary lesson from the church of Pergamos is that as children of God, we must never compromise with the world. We live in the world, but we must not be of the world. We are to be completely different from the world. Our pasts have been buried in Jesus Christ, and He keeps no record. We may have the same bodies with signs of age, but we do not have the same minds or the same hearts. Jesus has made us new creatures, sons and daughters of the living God. We are now children of the light. We are Christians. We praise God for what Jesus Christ has done, and is doing in our lives. Even though we often fail in what He wants us to do, and occasionally we get depressed, Jesus never fails us. That is the kind of God we serve.

Many people procrastinate in coming to Jesus because they think that they have to become perfect before they can approach Him. They will never make it on their own. Even as Christians, none of us will ever accomplish a state of perfection during this lifetime. The day we die, though, those of us who have made Jesus Christ the Lord of our lives, will enter into His presence, and will become perfect.

Jesus forgives us of every sin as we confess them to Him. He cleanses us; He washes us from all iniquity; He makes us brand new. He knows where we are right now. There is no reason *not* to open up to Him right now. There is nothing hidden from Him.

The Effect of God's Word

Other than what is said about Antipas in verse thirteen, Jesus has nothing good to say about the church of Pergamos. As with all seven of the letters in the book of Revelation, there are seven distinct sections that we will see: the commission, the character, the commendation, the condemnation, the correction, the call, and the challenge. The commission is in verse twelve, **And to the angel** [or the pastor] **of the church in Pergamos write, 'These things says He who has the sharp two-edged sword . . . .'**

Jesus Christ appears to the church of Pergamos with a sharp two-edged sword. British archaeologist Sir William Ramsay said, "In Roman estimation, the sword was a symbol of the highest order of official authority with which the pro consulate of Asia was invested. The right of the sword was roughly equivalent to what we call the power of life and death."

Spiritually speaking, the sword is the Word of God, sharply dividing between good and evil. Hebrews 4:12 graphically illustrates this principle, "For the word of God is living and powerful, and sharper than any two-edged sword, piercing even to the division of soul and spirit, and of joints and marrow, and is a discerner of the thoughts and intents of the heart." The two-edged sword in the letter to the church of Pergamos signifies that the character of Jesus

Christ is the Word of God.

Living in the Enemy's Camp

Notice Jesus' commendation in verse thirteen, **I know your works, and where you dwell, where Satan's throne is.** Literally, "I know where you live." They were living right in the middle of Satan's throne. They were living at the center of emperor worship in Asia Minor from where the Roman empire was being ruled.

Verse thirteen continues, **And you hold fast to My name, and did not deny My faith even in the days in which Antipas was My faithful martyr, who was killed among you, where Satan dwells.** We know nothing about Antipas outside of this passage of Scripture. Nevertheless, the Holy Spirit put him in this letter. Antipas probably never imagined that he would even be remembered at all, certainly not two thousand years later. As always, though, God saved Himself a remnant. Antipas did not deny his faith, even when it meant that he would have to die for Jesus Christ. Jesus teaches us in Matthew 16:24, "If anyone desires to come after Me, let him deny himself, and take up his cross, and follow Me. For whoever desires to save his life will lose it, and whoever loses his life for My sake will find it. For what is a man profited if he gains the whole world, and loses his own soul? Or what will a man give in exchange for his soul?" God always gives us the opportunity to accept His will, or reject it. Antipas chose the unpopular way of death, and God honored him for that choice.

Selling Out

The condemnation is stated in verse fourteen: **But I have a few things against you . . .** , that is, against those people who were compromising and living lives of worldliness. **. . . Because you have there those who hold the doctrine of Balaam, who taught Balak to put a stumbling block before the children of Israel, to eat things sacrificed to idols, and to commit sexual immorality.** The sin of Balaam (Numbers 22-24) is the sin of greed. King Balak came and offered Balaam money so that he would prophesy against the children of Israel. Ba-laam refused to comply, because he knew that God's penalty for false prophecy was death. But in order to make some money out of the deal, he brought some of the king's women down to the children of Israel, and had them seduce the children of Israel through idolatry and sexual immorality. In this way, Balaam sinned against God. Even though he knew God's holy nature, he compromised. The book of Numbers records that Balaam was killed in battle. He had been a prophet of God, but he sold out, and turned his back on God. He became an apostate against God.

There are a lot of people like Balaam who sell out cheaply. A prime example is Judas Iscariot. Judas walked with Jesus for over three years. He saw every miracle that Christ performed; he heard every word that Christ taught. He even experienced the power of the Holy Spirit in his own life when Jesus sent out the seventy to minister to the nearby towns. Yet, for the price of thirty pieces of silver, or about $220, Judas sold his eternal soul. How much is eternity worth to you? What can you gain in the seventy or so years on this earth that can compare with eternity?

A Stumbling Block to Others

Balaam, then, put a stumbling block in front of the children of Israel. The word stumbling block literally means, "to use a bait stick to catch something; like a trap, or a snare." Balaam used a snare to trap the children of Israel into sinning, by bringing idolatrous women into the camp. God cursed him because he betrayed the people of God. We have been given this account, not only in the Old Testament, but also in the message to the church of Pergamos, in order that we would learn from the sin of Balaam. Do not think that God's love and mercy will cancel out God's righteousness. God will judge sin, and His judgment is perfectly righteous. No one will get away with even the slightest sin. God's grace is absolutely fantastic, but He only pours it out upon those who repent and obey His Word. Even as Christians, we must be careful how we treat the grace of God.

Verse fifteen discloses yet another sin of this church, **Thus you also have those who hold the doctrine of the Nicolaitans, which thing I hate**. The doctrine of the Nicolaitans was initially mentioned in the letter to the church of Ephesus in Revelation 2:6. The Ephesian church refused to accept this doctrine, but here we see that it has made its way into the church of Pergamos. The Nicolaitans believed that priests should rule over the laity. They elevated the position of the clergy to a level that God never intended. They postulated that the people were unqualified to read the Bible for themselves, and that they could not approach God on their own. The pastorate became a profession, rather than a calling. Many still regard it as such today. Jesus, however, leaves little doubt as to what He thinks about a professional priesthood—He hates it.

The lesson from the church of Pergamos is that the sin of idolatry is quite serious in God's sight. God demands that we worship Him only, and He demands that our worship be on His terms only. This church began practices such as the worship of Mary, the worship of saints and of angels, the exaltation of the priesthood, praying for the dead, and all of these things that have grown inside the church like a cancer. They all amount to idolatry because they substitute man-made traditions for the Word of God.

The Choice is Ours

Notice the correction in verse sixteen, **Repent, or else I will come to you quickly and will fight against them with the sword of My mouth.** Jesus promises to use the two-edged sword against us if we continue in a lifestyle of sin. God will judge sin. He offers grace and love, but if we refuse those gifts, then He will destroy us. He has given us the choice. He wants a people that He can call His own; a people with whom He can fellowship. If we choose *not* to repent, then He will chasten us. He will repeatedly try to draw us to Himself, but eventually, if we refuse His overtures, there will come a point at which He will stop, and His righteous judgment will begin. On this earth, we have many second chances, but when this life is over, there are no more second chances. His judgment, as well as His grace, stands for eternity. It is our choice.

In verse seventeen is the call, **He who has an ear, let him hear what the Spirit says to the churches.** Just like in our churches today, there were a lot of people in the church of Pergamos who were given the Word of God, but did not hear; they were not listening. Is God's Spirit speaking to you as you read this? The Holy Spirit has come to convict the world of sin, to speak of righteousness, and to warn of judgment. It is very important that we hear the Word of the Holy Spirit, because Jesus Christ is coming again, first for His bride, the church, and then to judge the world. Are you ready to meet Him face to face?

There are three important observations in verse seventeen: First, **He who has an ear . . .** is a rebuke to those who call themselves Christians, yet seldom, if ever, read their Bibles, or pray to God. If you only pray during times of crisis, what does that say about your relationship with God? Secondly, everything touching our salvation depends on the giving of an attentive ear to the divine Word. We must make diligent use of our privileges to hear, to mark, to learn, and to inwardly digest God's Word. The Bible contains a personal message for each one of us, and we would be foolish to ignore it. Thirdly, everyone has the capacity to give attention, and so it is laid upon all of us to use that capacity to hear what the Spirit is saying to the churches. No one will be able to say, "Lord, I never heard."

Jesus Sustains Us

The challenge: **To him who overcomes I will give some of the hidden manna to eat. And I will give him a white stone, and on the stone a new name written which no one knows except him who receives it.** What is the hidden manna that we are promised? In John 6:35, Jesus told us, "I am the bread of life. He who comes to Me shall never hunger." When we come to Him, He becomes our

bread of life. He becomes real in our lives. He is the sus-
tenance by which we have eternal life.

In addition to the hidden manna, those who overcome
are promised a white stone, and on the stone a new name
written which no one knows except him who receives it.
The white stone and the black stone were used to deter-
mine the will of God in the Old Testament. The white
stone here is in reference to Jesus Christ accepting us as
His children. On it will be a new name that will be given
to us when we get to heaven. We have not received our
new names yet, although the Lord may reveal them to us at
any time. God's promises are incredible, and they are
given to every one of us who accept His grace. All we
must do is humble ourselves before Him, and say, "Lord,
here I am."

No Turning Back

The older I become, the more I realize that there is no
way I would want to go back to where I was before I knew
Jesus. I want to be prepared to see Him face to face. I
want to make sure that when the Lord calls me home, that I
can stand before Him, and hear Him say, "Well done, good
and faithful servant. Come in, and see what I have prepared for you!"

The Bible has many awesome warnings concerning
the ultimate outcome of those who reject Jesus Christ.
Jesus Himself taught that hell is a place of weeping and
gnashing of teeth, where people are tormented day and
night with an unquenchable fire. The smoke of their torment ascends forever and ever, and they have no rest. In
this life, we perceive death to be at least a temporary es-

cape from our torment; but in hell, there is no such escape.
The worm does not die, and the fire is never quenched
throughout all eternity. Take a close look at Jesus' words
in Matthew 24:48-51, Revelation 14:9-11, and Mark 9:43-
48. Contrast those Scriptures with Jesus' words for those
who have made Him their Lord and Master in John 14:2-3,
"In My Father's house are many mansions; if it were not
so, I would have told you. I go to prepare a place for you.
And if I go and prepare a place for you, I will come again
and receive you to Myself; that where I am, there you may
be also."

Revelation 21-22 give us the picture of heaven as a
place of comfort, where we will be with our Lord and
Savior Jesus Christ forever. There will be no more death,
no more tears, no more sorrow; only love, joy, and peace.
That is where the child of God is going; that is where our
hope is.

FIVE

THE LETTER TO THE CHURCH OF THYATIRA

(Revelation 2:18-29)

"And to the angel of the church in Thyatira write, 'These things says the Son of God, who has eyes like a flame of fire, and His feet like fine brass: I know your works, love, service, faith, and your patience; and as for your works, the last are more than the first. Nevertheless I have a few things against you, because you allow that woman Jezebel, who calls herself a prophetess, to teach and beguile My servants to commit sexual immorality and to eat things sacrificed to idols. And I gave her time to repent of her sexual immorality, and she did not repent. Indeed I will cast her into a sickbed, and those who commit adultery with her into great tribulation, unless they repent of their deeds. And I will kill her children with death. And all the churches shall know that I am He who searches the minds and hearts. And I will give to each one of you according to your works. But to you I say, and to the rest in Thyatira, as many as do not have this doctrine, and who have not known the depths of Satan, as they call them, I will put on you no other burden.

But hold fast what you have till I come. And he who overcomes, and keeps My works until the end, to him I will give power over the nations–He shall rule them with a rod of iron; as the potter's vessels shall be broken to pieces–as I also have received from My Father; and I will give him the morning star. He who has an ear, let him hear what the Spirit says to the churches.' "

-5-

The church of Thyatira is the corrupted church. This is a pagan church. It began about A.D. 606, and will continue through the Great Tribulation, until the Second Coming of Jesus Christ. The letter to the church of Thyatira is the longest of any to the seven churches, and the doctrine held by this church is probably the most critical of the seven. The name Thyatira means "continual sacrifice."

This is the only church of the seven in which a woman is seen as a prophetess, or as a pastor. In every recorded instance in which Jesus spoke of women, the application was to evil rather than to good. Jesus uses the example of Jezebel in this letter. Jezebel was the wife of Ahab, a wicked king of Israel who reigned from about 900 to 850 B.C. She killed many prophets of the Lord, and she introduced idolatry into the nation of Israel. Jezebel has become a type of the Roman Catholic Church. For a good background on the correlation between the Roman Catholic Church and the idolatry of ancient Babylon read *The Two Babylons* by Alexander Hislop (Loizeaux Brothers Publishers).

The city of Thyatira was founded in the early fourth century by Seleucid I, although some evidence indicates that it may have been founded by Alexander the Great a century earlier. Geographically, Thyatira was located ap-

proximately 30 miles southeast of Pergamos, and 30 miles
northwest of Sardis. Historically, the cities of Ephesus,
Smyrna, and Pergamos were much more notable than Thyatira. Biblically, Thyatira is first mentioned in connection
with Paul's second missionary journey in Acts 16:14. His
first convert in Europe was a woman of Thyatira by the
name of Lydia. She was a seller of purple cloth, a com-
modity for which the city of Thyatira was famous throughout the ancient world. It is believed that the church of
Thyatira was begun either by Lydia, or perhaps by evange-
lization from the believers in Ephesus.

A Church of Works

The most prominent characteristic of the church of
Thyatira was its man-made works, rather than doctrinal
understanding. The primary emphasis was on its own
achievements, as opposed to relying on Jesus Christ. The
church was not nearly as concerned with the teaching of
biblical doctrine as it was in maintaining its own traditions.
The historical church of Thyatira produced what is known
in history as the Dark Ages, a time when Christianity
knowingly and wantonly merged with paganism. This had
begun in the church of Pergamos during the reign of Constantine, and continued through the Reformation. During
this period of church history, many so-called "Christian"
doctrines were established through a compromise of biblical doctrines and pagan teachings. The result was man-
made religion. The following is a list of the doctrinal high-
lights of the church of Thyatira, the Roman Catholic
Church:

-Title of pope given to Boniface III by emperor Phocas
 (A.D. 607)

-Doctrine of kissing the pope's foot (A.D. 709)

-Worship of the cross, images, and relics authorized
 (A.D. 786)

-Use of holy water (A.D. 850)

-Canonization of dead saints by Pope John XV (A.D.
 995)

-Fasting on Fridays during Lent (A.D. 998)

-Celibacy of the priesthood by pope Gregory VII;
 priests and nuns forbidden to marry (A.D. 1079)

-Mechanical praying with beads, or the Rosary,
 invented by Peter the Hermit (A.D. 1090)

-The Inquisition (A.D. 1184)

-Sale of indulgences (A.D. 1190)

-Transubstantiation established (A.D. 1215)

-Establishment of the communion wafer (A.D. 1220)

-The Bible forbidden to laymen; only the priest could
 read the Bible; he would inform the people of
 God's message (A.D. 1229)

-Communion cup forbidden to the people (A.D. 1414).

-Doctrine of purgatory decreed by Council of Florence
 (A.D. 1439)

-Seven sacraments affirmed, including baptism,
 penance, holy communion, confirmation, holy mat-
 rimony, holy orders, and extreme unction (A.D.
 1439)

-*Ave Maria* approved (A.D. 1508)

-Jesuit priesthood order founded by Ignatius Loyola
 (A.D. 1534)

-Roman Catholic tradition granted equal authority
 with the Bible (A.D. 1545)

-Apocrypha books added to the Bible by the Council
   of Trent; these books are not accepted as inspired
   literature by the Protestant movement, however,
   they do contain some useful historical information
   (A.D. 1546)
-Immaculate Conception of Mary introduced (A.D.
   1854)
-Syllabus of Errors proclaimed by Vatican Council
   (A.D. 1864)
-Infallibility of the pope declared (A.D. 1870).
-Public schools condemned by Pius XI (A.D. 1930).
-Assumption of the Virgin Mary proclaimed by Pius
   XII (A.D. 1950)
-Mary proclaimed to be the Mother of the Church by
   Paul VI (A.D. 1965).

The Reformation

Martin Luther, a Roman Catholic monk in the early
sixteenth century, tried desperately to satisfy the require-
ments of the Roman Catholic Church by nearly starving
himself to death, and beating himself into unconsciousness
in a regular ritual of penance and contrition. He felt that
by abusing his body, he could atone for his sins. Despite
these fanatical measures of penance, though, he never quite
felt satisfied that he had earned forgiveness from God. In
his frustration, he was ready to leave the priesthood and
give up his faith in God altogether. He realized that there
was nothing he could do to eradicate his sin. Finally, while
reading the book of Romans, the doctrine of justification
by faith alone hit him like a bolt of lightning.

In 1517, Luther wrote his now famous Ninety-five

point Theses, and nailed it to the door of the Wittenberg church in Germany. His theses detailed ninety-five false teachings of the Roman Catholic Church. He was promptly excommunicated. That was the beginning of the Reformation.

False Teachings

As mentioned, the name Thyatira means "continual sacrifice." One of the greatest heresies of the Roman Catholic Church, through its rituals, traditions, and practices, is the denial of the finished work of Jesus Christ. The belief in a continual sacrifice for the remission of sins, which produced such things as the Mass, which also means "sacrifice," the sacraments, praying for the dead, and burning of candles, directly contradicts Scripture. Hebrews 9:24-28 gives a pointed commentary on the subject:

> For Christ has not entered the holy places made with hands, which are copies of the true, but into heaven itself, now to appear in the presence of God for us; not that He should offer Himself often, as the high priest enters the Most Holy Place every year with blood of another–He then would have had to suffer often since the foundation of the world; but now, once at the end of the ages, He has appeared to put away sin by the sacrifice of Himself. And as it is appointed for men to die once, but after this the judgment, so Christ was offered once to bear the sins of many. To those who eagerly wait for Him He will appear a second time, apart from sin, for salvation.

Another false teaching of the Roman Catholic Church is the system of indulgences, or special graces granted by the church in exchange for money. This teaching and practice was authorized and abused widely by Leo X around 1516-17. People would come to a priest and negotiate the price of forgiveness for their sins, or for the early release of loved ones from Purgatory (another false teaching). The church propagated the notion that there was a certain amount that every person would have to pay in order to have all of his sins forgiven for the rest of his life. After tendering the given sum, they basically could live anyway they wanted. They were assured falsely of the gift of eternal life by a corrupt religious system, instead of a true assurance through a personal relationship with Jesus Christ. The church, needless to say, became extremely rich from the practice of indulgences, to the point, among other things, that it was able to build St. Peter's Basilica in Rome.

Another false teaching of the Roman Catholic Church is that the pope is infallible, or in matters of faith and doctrine, the pope can make no mistakes. The pope is a human being, just like any one of us, and as flesh, is capable of making mistakes in every area of his life. As a man, he also comes under the conviction of Romans 3:23, "For all have sinned and fall short of the glory of God."

In instances recorded in the book of Revelation, the Apostle John, so overcome with joy over certain occurrences in heaven, drops to his knees before the angel of God. Each time he is sternly rebuked. Worship is only to be given to God, he is told. The ritual of kissing the pope's ring, then, or bowing to him, or paying homage to him, or to any man, is equally blasphemous (see Romans 1:18-25).

All heresy falls into one of two categories: 1) the denial of the deity and personal lordship of Jesus Christ;

2) the addition of any requirement for salvation other than faith in the shed blood of Jesus Christ.

The Roman Catholic Church is guilty of diluting God's salvation by grace alone, because it does not believe or teach the sufficiency of Christ's sacrifice for sin once and for all. Their ritual Mass celebrates the crucifixion of Jesus Christ over and over again. Even their crucifix depicting the body of a dead Christ hanging on it undermines His glorious resurrection. Jesus Christ sits at the right hand of God the Father interceding for the saints—the *living* saints. To keep Him on the cross, or as a baby in His mother's arms, or as a child on the shoulder of Christopher, is heresy.

A Leader During the Tribulation

The church of Thyatira will continue into the Great Tribulation. The Bible says that in the last days there will come an antichrist and a false prophet. The Antichrist will be the world political leader, and the false prophet will be the world religious leader. In order for the world to be brought under a single ruling government and a single religion, the major religions, most likely led by the Roman Catholic Church and the World Council of Churches, will come to some type of ecumenical agreement. This world ecumenical movement has been a top priority of Pope John Paul II.

Message of Judgment

The message in the letter to the church of Thyatira is one of judgment. The commission is given in verse eighteen: **And to the angel of the church in Thyatira write, 'These things says the Son of God, who has eyes like a flame of fire, and His feet like fine brass . . . .'** Jesus represents Himself as the Son of God, with piercing eyes that burn deep into the soul. His feet are like fine brass. In the Scriptures, brass is always symbolic of judgment. Silver speaks of redemption, and gold of deity. It is important to keep in mind that Jesus Christ is aware of what is going on in His church at all times, and His awareness brings judgment if there is no repentance.

Blind Leaders of the Blind

The commendation is given in verse nineteen: **I know your works, love, service, faith, and your patience; and as for your works, the last are more than the first.** This is a characteristic description of the Roman Catholic Church. It is an extremely hard-working church. The faithfulness of its people cannot be questioned. However, their faithfulness is to the church itself, and not to the living Savior of the Bible, the risen Lord, Jesus Christ. The people are faithful to a system of works, not to a Savior of grace. They are deceived by the Roman Catholic leaders who "shut up the kingdom of heaven against men" because they neither go in themselves, nor "allow those who are entering to go in" (Matthew 23:13). Jesus is displeased with their system, and with those who have deceived the people and have kept them from the truth of God's Word.

Many priests in the Roman Catholic Church have never accepted Jesus Christ as their personal Lord and Savior. They are heathens serving in churches. This is sad, but true. There are plenty of heathen pastors in Prot-

estant churches as well. There are multitudes of non-
Christians in seminaries all over the world. God is aware
of what is going on in His church, and He will bring judgment.

Idolatry and Sexual Immorality

The condemnation comes in verse twenty: **Nevertheless I have a few things against you, because you allow
that woman Jezebel, who calls herself a prophetess, to
teach and beguile My servants to commit sexual immorality and to eat things sacrificed to idols.** The
church is following its leaders, rather than checking on
what God has to say in His Word. They are obeying the
system, but they are not obeying God. This woman Jezebel, the religious system, is causing the people to commit
two grievous sins: acts of sexual immorality, and eating
meat that has been sacrificed to idols—in short, sexual and
spiritual immorality.

Idolatry has spread throughout the church. Depictions
of Mary suffering as co-redemptrix are completely blasphemous. There is only one Redeemer—Jesus Christ
(1 Timothy 2:5). Mary has nothing to do with our redemption. Mary was a beautiful woman who, as a virgin, bore
Jesus Christ. She then married Joseph, had normal sexual
relations, and bore other children after Jesus. Matthew
13:55-56 lists Jesus' brothers, and then mentions that He
had sisters as well.

The Old Testament book of 1 Kings records that Jezebel killed the prophets of God, and brought idolatry to the
children of Israel by seducing them into worshiping the
god Baal. The church of Thyatira has been guilty of much

bloodshed in the name of Jesus Christ. The Crusaders during the early Middle Ages blessed the people, and slaughtered the Jews. Church history is an absolute disgrace. We learn from church history what *not* to do. The only relevant history of the church is its interaction with Jesus Christ. Nothing else will matter ultimately.

Opportunity to Repent

God's grace and patience is revealed in verse twenty-one: **And I gave her time to repent of her sexual immorality, and she did not repent.** God gives man ample opportunity to repent of his immorality, but man stubbornly clings to his way of death, leaving no choice but judgment. Verse twenty-two announces the judgment: **Indeed I will cast her into a sickbed, and those who commit adultery with her into great tribulation, unless they repent of their deeds.** If the people who are in the Roman Catholic system do not come out, repent, and accept Jesus Christ as their Lord and Savior, they will find themselves living on earth during the Great Tribulation because of their sin.

Grace in Judgment

And I will kill her children with death. And all the churches shall know that I am He who searches the minds and hearts. And I will give to each one of you according to your works. God is angry with the sin in the world. He will search the minds and the hearts of every man. God knows the motives behind our works. If we are truly saved by faith in Jesus Christ, then our lives will show it by true works. We are not saved by works; we are saved by faith in Jesus Christ. Salvation is the gift of God. We cannot be saved by going to church, or by keeping the Sabbath, or by keeping all of the church traditions. Jesus Christ alone saves us.

Jesus gives words of comfort in verses twenty-four and twenty-five to those who are faithful and true believers: **But to you I say, and to the rest in Thyatira, as many as do not have this doctrine, and who have not known the depths of Satan, as they call them, I will put on you no other burden. But hold fast what you have till I come.** Even though He is bringing judgment, Jesus assures us that there are some who will escape the judgment. There are some who have not placed tradition above God's Word in their hearts. Jesus encourages them, "Hold fast." He is coming soon.

Hope for the Overcomer

And he who overcomes, and keeps My works until the end, to him I will give power over the nations–He shall rule them with a rod of iron; as the potter's vessels shall be broken to pieces–as I also have received from My Father; and I will give him the morning star. Those who hold on to the truth of Jesus Christ, and do not get involved with sexual and spiritual immorality, will be given power over the nations. The church of Jesus Christ will reign over the nations in the Kingdom Age.

He who has an ear, let him hear what the Spirit says to the churches. Listen to what Jesus Christ has to say; He wants to live inside your heart.

SIX

The Letter to the
Church of Sardis

(Revelation 3:1-6)

"And to the angel of the church in Sardis write, 'These things says He who has the seven Spirits of God and the seven stars: I know your works, that you have a name that you are alive, but you are dead. Be watchful, and strengthen the things which remain, that are ready to die, for I have not found your works perfect before God. Remember therefore how you have received and heard; hold fast and repent. Therefore if you will not watch, I will come upon you as a thief, and you will not know what hour I will come upon you. You have a few names even in Sardis who have not defiled their garments; and they shall walk with Me in white, for they are worthy. He who overcomes shall be clothed in white garments, and I will not blot out his name from the Book of Life; but I will confess his name before My Father and before His angels. He who has an ear, let him hear what the Spirit says to the churches.' "

-6-

The church of Sardis is known as the "dead church." It began in about A.D. 1520 with the advent of the Reformation, and will continue into the Great Tribulation. Sardis means "escaping once," or "a remnant." Even though Sardis is a dead church, its history had been great.

At one time the Greeks had regarded Sardis as the greatest of all cities. Its coins, the oldest of all known coins, bore the proud inscription, "Sardis, the first metropolis of Asia, and of Lydia, and of the Helenism." Sardis was the most important manufacturing center in the early Lydian kingdom. The city probably dates back to about 1200 B.C. with the beginning of the kingdom of Lydia. It was located about 65 miles east of Smyrna, and about 30 miles southeast of Thyatira.

Sardis was built on a small plateau ranging from 950 to 1,500 feet in height. It was a war-torn city. Cyrus the Great, king of Persia, captured it from a fabulously rich king by the name of Croesus, and then in 546 B.C. the city was re-taken by the Persians. Sardis was represented by a deity who was believed to have the power to restore people back from the dead. The Athenians burned the city in 490 B.C., and in 334 B.C., it was surrendered to Alexander the Great of Macedonia. Antiochus the Great (not Antiochus Epiphanes), king of Syria, conquered it in 214 B.C., and then lost it to the Romans in 190 B.C. Finally in A.D. 17, it was destroyed by an earthquake, and even though rebuilt, it was never restored to its former glory. In the fourteenth century, it was destroyed by the Turks. Today, it exists as a tiny city with few inhabitants.

The Protestant Church

There are some tremendous insights in this letter to the church of Sardis. First, the church of Sardis is referred to as the dead church, although that was not always the case. The church of Sardis is the church of the Protestant Reformation. The Reformation was brought about by a reaction to the pagan worship that was going on within the Roman Catholic Church in the name of Christ. When Luther, Calvin, Zwingli, Wesley, and others rose up and rebelled against the heresies of the Roman Catholic Church, God began to reform His Church. Martin Luther's Ninety-five Theses marked the beginning of the Protestant movement, and eventually he, and many others were excommunicated from the Roman Catholic Church for their beliefs.

The driving force behind the Protestant Reformation was the people's intolerance of the old system. The Roman Catholic Church had combined God's Word with its own man-made traditions. The Roman Catholic leaders took the true worship of God, and turned it into a religion. God will not tolerate people attempting to put Him in a box. True worship of God is governed by God, not by man. When people set up a religious system, then by definition, it is governed by man. Throughout history, no religious system devised by man has ever led people to God.

When man attempts to dictate worship, God simply begins a new work elsewhere.

The leaders of the Reformation were on fire for God, and their fire brought revival to the church. The revival, though, was far from permanent. God always begins spiritual revival where there is spiritual stagnation, because the people are hungry for an authentic relationship with Him. Even within the revival though, if people begin to set up their own rules, rather than continuing to rely upon God for guidance, then they still end up putting God into a box of their own, and the revival is quenched. God then goes elsewhere and begins another revival among people who are hungry to know Him on His terms.

For several hundred years, the Protestant Reformation brought new life into the church, but characteristic of man's historical interaction with God, the church eventually got too comfortable with the way things were being done. They established their own traditions, which soon began to take precedence over the leading of the Holy Spirit, and they lost their spiritual edge, or sensitivity to the Holy Spirit. By the nineteenth century, Liberalism began to encroach.

Liberalism

This move toward Liberalism began in Germany, where the Germans prided themselves in their great rational thinking. These German theologians were highly intellectual, but spiritually dead. Whatever could not be proven scientifically was dismissed as religious folklore. They discarded as absurd the doctrines of the inerrancy of Scripture, the Virgin Birth, the Deity of Christ, the substitutionary atonement of Christ, and the bodily death, resurrection, ascension and second coming of Christ. These men were not atheists, but they certainly did not believe in the God of the Bible. They introduced into the church a thoroughly humanistic form of religion called "Liberal Christianity."

In order to share in the prestige of the German theological community, the Protestant churches in the United States began sending their young pastors to the seminaries in Germany. When these young pastors came back, they were completely indoctrinated in the liberal mindset. Rather than just getting rid of these young aberrant theologians, the denominations, instead, hired them to teach in their seminaries.

With this intellectual brand of theology, certain seminaries such as Harvard, Yale, and Princeton quickly developed prestigious reputations among the denominations. The move toward Liberalism began with the Southern Baptists, the Methodists, and the Lutherans, but it eventually spread throughout the entire Protestant church, and has continued to the present day in most of the major seminaries across the United States. In the first verse of Revelation 3, Jesus Christ proclaims that they are dead.

Inerrancy of Scripture

The inspiration and inerrancy of the Bible is the central issue of the entire discrepancy between conservative Christianity, Liberalism, and what has recently come to be known as Neo-Orthodoxy. The significance placed on God's Word determines every other doctrine of Christianity. Atheists, agnostics, and cultists have discredited the validity of the Bible for millennia, but one of the most serious problems facing the church of Jesus Christ today, is the great number of people within the church who believe and teach that the Bible can be trusted only in a limited way. They claim that the Bible as a whole is inspired by God, although not every part of it is true; that the Bible is trustworthy concerning theological and moral issues, but in the areas of science and history there are deficiencies. They believe that God inspired the broad concepts of the Bible, but since He left the actual words up to the individuals who wrote them, the details cannot be fully trusted. The Bible has some good advice, but it also has its problems.

The simple problem with this approach is that if the Bible cannot be completely trusted as the Word of God, then which parts are incorrect? No one can agree, so, consequently, there are hundreds of Protestant denominations all over the country, each believing something slightly different from the other. Many of these churches even believe that their particular denomination will be the only one to gain heaven. The church is sick because it has discarded the truth of God's Word.

The Bible did not come down through the ages from printing presses; it was copied by hand, one letter at a time. The scribes would start from the book of Genesis, and copy word for word from an existing copy. The duty of the scribe was considered sacred, especially when it came to writing the name of God. The name of God was so holy to these men, that every time the copyist would write the name of God, he would wash his pen, bathe himself, put on a clean set of clothing, and then resume writing. Imagine the labor involved copying some of the passages in which the name of God is found over thirty times! Understanding the grueling nature of the copyist's job, and the absolute diligence that these men exercised in transcribing the Bible, we can appreciate the miracle of the Book that we now hold in our hands. Some of these men labored their entire lifetimes copying the Scriptures.

However, the manuscripts of the Bible available to us today contain some copyist errors. We do not claim that every copy of the Bible is perfect; we claim that the original version that God inspired was perfect. For instance, 2 Chronicles 22:2 lists Ahaziah as being forty-two years-old when he became king. Second Kings 8:26 lists him as being twenty-two years-old. In 2 Chronicles 9:25, Solomon had four thousand horse stalls, and in 1 Kings 4:26, he had forty thousand. It is important to point out, however, that although there are copyist errors, they are rare. There are not hundreds of errors in the Bible, and in most cases we know the correct answer. For instance, we know that Solomon had four thousand stalls rather than forty thousand, by comparing how many horses he had, and we know that Ahaziah was twenty-two years old, not forty-two years old, because if he had been forty-two years-old, he would have been four years older than his father. Moreover, in no case does a copyist error affect any doctrine of Scripture.

Suppose you received a telegram that read: "_OU HAVE WON $5,000.00." You would not hesitate to claim your award, even though due to the copyist error, you cannot be absolutely certain that the notice refers to you as the winner.

Now suppose you received another copy that read: "Y_U HAVE WON $5,000.00." This would make you even more certain, although it also contains an error. How do two errors make you more sure than one error? Because the error is in a different place.

You would easily be able to sort out all of the errors, because every version gives you another verification of every other word in the text. We have 5,366 manuscripts in the Greek language of the New Testament, so the copyist errors in the manuscripts are of little significance.

However, there cannot be an error in any of the original manuscripts because God cannot err. The Bible is based on the authenticity of God the Father; it has been given the personal authority of Jesus Christ, and it was inspired through individual men by the in-breathing of the Holy Spirit. Therefore, if you were to claim that there was even one error in the Bible, it would be an attack on the authenticity of God the Father, the authority of God the Son, and the ministry of God the Holy Spirit.

Furthermore, the unexplained is not necessarily unexplainable. If we studied the Bible over the course of our entire lifetime, we still would not be able to explain every problem found in it because we are not God. We are not infinite; there are definite limits to our knowledge. Likewise, no scientist can explain everything in nature. There are anomalies, or differences, in nature that no one has ever been able to figure out. What they do not know, they study all the more diligently. Just the same, the things we do not understand in the Bible need to be studied all the more diligently.

Nevertheless, we must temper our study of the mysteries of the Bible with this observation by Mark Twain: "It's not the parts of the Bible I cannot understand which cause me the most difficulty. It's what I can understand that causes me the most difficulty." No one can understand what the seven thunders are uttered in Revelation 10:4 because God commanded the Apostle John to seal them up.

Everyone, though, can understand what was spoken by the thunderous voice on Mount Sinai when it said, "Thou shalt not kill." The main things in the Bible are the plain things. We should not be discouraged or frustrated by the verses we cannot understand, but rather, spend our time on the verses that we can understand.

Understanding the incredible task of preserving the integrity of God's Word down through the centuries, we can appreciate why the leaders of the Reformation, as well as those in subsequent generations all over the world, gave their lives to maintain the teaching of the Bible in the church. Even today, although there are many liberal and neo-orthodox theologians who do not give the people the full counsel of Jesus Christ, God still maintains a remnant of conservative Christian scholars who are battling to teach nothing else but the Bible in the church.

Fullness of the Holy Spirit

In His letter to the church of Sardis, God is pleading with the church. Jesus Christ is represented in verse one as **He who has the seven Spirits of God and the seven stars.** What are the seven Spirits of God? Seven is the number of completion, so the seven-fold Spirit of God is the manifestation of the Holy Spirit in His fullness. Isaiah 11:1-2 describes the seven Spirits of God: "There shall come forth a Rod from the stem of Jesse, and a Branch shall grow out of his roots. The Spirit of the LORD shall rest upon Him, the Spirit of wisdom and understanding, the Spirit of counsel and might, the Spirit of knowledge and of the fear of the LORD."

Jesus Christ approaches this church in the fullness of

His Holy Spirit, but the people of this church are trying to do God's work in the power of the flesh. The church must be led by the Holy Spirit because God's work cannot be done without His anointing. Yet, look at the church today. So many pastors run their churches from one program to the next. Where does God fit in? The pastors see no need for God because their committees make all the important decisions. They stumble along, trying to please as many people as possible in their congregations, especially the wealthy ones, rather than simply teaching God's Word and letting the Holy Spirit do His ministry of teaching, convicting, and guiding. The pastors write and read books, and give and attend seminars on church growth while relying on their annual pledge drives to meet the budget. Most men in the clergy have no calling from God. They attend seminary to pursue the ministry, and they become professionals instead of pastors. They are not true shepherds; they are merely hirelings. They have no desire in their hearts for the Word of God, and they really do not even want to minister to the people of God. They are simply filling the position in order to put bread on the table. How sad it is!

This is the church of Sardis—the Protestant church of today. God says to them, "I did a real work in this church, but as I blessed you, instead of worshipping me as your Supplier, you attributed the success to your demographic studies. You have denied My Word, and you have brought pagan customs into My church." This is the case with most, if not all, mainline denominations. God does a work within the church, people come to know Jesus Christ, and lives are radically changed. The flame generally lasts no more than one generation. People begin to lose the excitement of the power of God in their lives; they become insensitive to the conviction of the Holy Spirit. Before long, sin is brought into the church. Soon, carnality is rampant within the church, and then everything is done in the power of the flesh. God's Spirit is gone, and the spirit of the church is dead.

We all need to pray for our churches—that God will continue the work that He has started, especially for the sake of the young people. We need to maintain that fire in our hearts. As time passes, the young people of today grow older, and everything constantly changes. If the Lord tarries, where will our relationships with Him be in the next ten years? We need to examine our lives everyday. The only way to be sure that we will finish the race is to continually move forward in the power of the Holy Spirit. If we are trying to maintain our relationships with Jesus Christ through another person, or based on another person's relationship with Jesus Christ, what will happen to your commitment if that other person stops serving the Lord? In this letter to the church of Sardis, God says, "Here I am in the fullest manifestation, showing you that I am God."

Spiritual Death

Jesus declares, I **know your works, that you have a name that you are alive, but you are dead.** This church is spiritually dead because they are living in the flesh. The people in the church of Sardis were being governed by their own wants and desires, rather than by the leading of the Holy Spirit. They care more about the things that will make their own lives comfortable here and now, rather than about the things that will enhance their relationship with Jesus Christ, or bring people into the kingdom of God.

What becomes of a church that is spiritually dead? The country of Great Britain is a perfect example of the tragic consequence. They have many magnificent cathedrals, where at one time, six and eight thousand people were hearing God's Word every single night. Now, twenty-five people on a Sunday morning is considered a great turnout. Many of those great cathedrals, too, have been converted into Muslim mosques. What a tragedy! It is a frightening thought that God would remove His Holy Spirit from a church that was once on fire for Him. That church would be left with only memories of past glories. The church, however, cannot afford to live in the past if it is to grow spiritually to have a godly impact on society.

Many churches in the United States today are filled with people who come to hear a social gospel—people who go to church so that they can dress up and impress others. Guys go to church to meet women, and women to meet guys. The fact that a church is packed on Sunday morning is not an indication of that church's spiritual life. The bigger the congregation, the easier for a person to hide, but if God is in the church, then the Holy Spirit will bring conviction of sin. A person may be able to hide among people, but he cannot hide from God. This is the message of Jesus: "I know your works."

Repentance as the Key

Jesus gives the admonition in verse two, **Be watchful, and strengthen the things which remain, that are ready to die, for I have not found your works perfect**

before God. The result of living to satisfy a carnal appetite is spiritual death. What must we do to remedy our condition? Repent. Get right with God. Begin to rebuild. Strengthen the spiritual part of your life that remains. Go into the sanctuary of your heart, and clean it up, just as Hezekiah did in 2 Kings 18. After all of the idolatry in the land, when Hezekiah was crowned king of Judah, he and his men went into the temple, removed all of the pagan idols, took them outside, and burned them. They got right with God. That is what God wants from us. God says to us, "If you want to fellowship with me, then get your life right."

Verse three exhorts us, **Remember therefore how you have received and heard; hold fast and repent.** In other words, Do you remember when you first heard the Word of God, and repented from your evil ways, and the Holy Spirit came into your life? Repent, and get back to that." Repentance is the key to this church's problems. The only way God can work through us is if we truly repent. God patiently tells the church of Sardis, "You can sit there and play the game of church all you want, but you are dead; and if you would honestly examine your heart, you would know that you are dead."

God used the men who led the Reformation to shake His church because they were committed to living for Him. If we are not absolutely consecrated to God, then God will not use us. If we seek positions in ministry in order to receive some form of authority or notoriety, then we will reap no spiritual benefit at all because God sees into the depths of our hearts. The Reformation began as a work of God, but ended up as an ecclesiastical system. What began as the work of the Spirit, has concluded as the work of the flesh (Galatians 3:3).

As pastors organize their systems, boards, and committees to run the church, they not only commit spiritual suicide, they quench the working of the Holy Spirit in their churches. God will not bless the work when man takes control; He will go somewhere else. God will accomplish His work with or without us. God spoke through a donkey in the Old Testament, so He certainly does not need any of us in order to accomplish His will. God even uses evil for good. Out of all of the corruption of the Roman Catholic Church, God brought the incredible spiritual revival of the Reformation. Then when the Protestant movement also sank into the mire of man's traditions, God produced spiritual revival elsewhere. He raised up men like Charles Spurgeon, D.L. Moody, and Billy Sunday. Even today, God has men who are bringing forth His Gospel in truth, men like Billy Graham, Chuck Smith, and John MacArthur.

God will always have a remnant of people who are willing to give their lives completely to His service. God's people will never be a majority, but neither will they ever be eradicated by the powers of evil. Liberal theologians definitely comprise the majority of the present-day church, however, those who hold fast to the Word of God are a tenacious minority. The size of the team has no bearing on who wins in the end. As the Apostle Paul triumphantly declares in Romans 8:31, "What then shall we say to these things? If God is for us, who can be against us?"

The Lordship of Christ

The second portion of verse three is an awesome warning: **Therefore if you will not watch, I will come**

upon you as a thief, and you will not know what hour I will come upon you. If we are not honestly serving Jesus Christ with our whole lives, then when He comes, we will not be ready. When Jesus comes for His faithful, He is coming to take them home, but for all others, He comes to bring His judgment. We are not Christians just because we were sprinkled as infants, or because we are on a church roll somewhere, or even because we went forward at an altar call at a particular moment in our lives. In order to truly be a Christian, a person must make Jesus Christ the absolute sovereign Lord of his life. When we use the title Lord in regard to Jesus Christ, it implies that we are His property, just as slaves are the property of their masters. We must give Christ complete control of every area of our lives. Jesus said that we shall be known by our fruits. What kind of fruit is being born from your life right now?

The Straight and Narrow Way

Jesus continues in verse four, **You have a few names even in Sardis who have not defiled their garments; and they shall walk with Me in white, for they are worthy.** Even in the dead church, there are a few who have not gone the way of spiritual death; but there are not many. Jesus said that the path which leads to the kingdom of God is very straight and narrow, and there are very few who follow it; but the way to destruction is very wide, and many go that way. Many are called, but few are chosen.

The narrowness of God's calling is evident throughout the Scriptures. Jesus issues a stern warning in Matthew 18:1-6, "At that time the disciples came to Jesus, saying, 'Who then is greatest in the kingdom of heaven?' And

Jesus called a little child to Him, set him in the midst of them, and said, 'Assuredly, I say to you, unless you are converted and become as little children, you will by no means enter the kingdom of heaven. Therefore whoever humbles himself as this little child is the greatest in the kingdom of heaven. And whoever receives one little child like this in My name receives Me. But whoever causes one of these little ones who believe in Me to sin, it would be better for him if a millstone were hung around his neck, and he were drowned in the depth of the sea.' " Those who teach children, whether as parents, or in a formal class-room setting, or simply as role models, have an awesome responsibility before God to train them in the ways of God.

The millstone was a massive round stone with a hole in the center. In Jesus' time, they used it for crushing grain to make bread, or olives for olive oil, or grapes for wine. The stone weighed two to four thousand pounds. Jesus tells us here that if someone would cause a child of God to sin, it would be better for him to take this stone, tie a rope around his neck, and cast it into the depths of the sea. The reference here is to eternal damnation.

Another application of Jesus' teaching in Matthew is that the child represents a person who has just accepted Jesus Christ as his Lord and Savior. The new Christian is like a little child spiritually. The wrath of God will be poured out upon anyone who would try to destroy that person's faith, or would lead him down a path that would re-sult in sin.

Paul tells us in the book of Romans that we can de-stroy people's faith in Jesus Christ by the way we live. Have you ever considered that? When we claim to be Christians, and then live as heathens, and are seen by a less mature Christian, and our actions cause him to sin, then we have misrepresented God. Moses misrepresented God to the people of Israel on one occasion, and God's punishment was to forbid him from entering the Promised Land. Moses represented God as being angry with the people, and when they needed water, instead of speaking to the rock, as God had commanded him, he beat the rock with his staff. As minor as this incident sounds, Moses' sin was that he misrepresented God, and God punished him severely for it.

Representatives of Christ

Consider the implications in our own lives. When we claim to be Christians by our words or actions, those around us who are not Christians will experience the conviction of the Holy Spirit. Because we profess a lifestyle that is radically different than theirs, they will feel uncomfortable. In order to soothe their own wounded consciences, they will search our lives with a magnifying glass in order to find some hypocrisy that will excuse their own sin.

As Christians, we have been given the awesome responsibility of representing God to the people around us. For example, if we react poorly to a stressful situation on the job, and our words or actions turn someone away from Jesus Christ who might have been just about ready to come to Him, then God holds us personally responsible.

Jesus told the parable of the man who began to build a house. Before he could finish the project, the man ran out of money, so he quit building. The half-finished structure served as a monument to this man's stupidity. From then on he was ridiculed by everyone who passed by. If we profess Jesus Christ as Lord and Savior, but are not willing to pay the price of following Him, we are the ones who are discredited, by man and by God.

How many people have been turned off from Jesus Christ because of the misrepresentation of God in the church today? Notice the consequences that Jesus teaches in Matthew 18:7-9: "Woe to the world because of offenses! For offenses must come, but woe to that man by whom the offense comes! And if your hand or foot causes you to sin, cut it off and cast it from you. It is better for you to enter into life lame or maimed, rather than having two hands or two feet, to be cast into the everlasting fire. And if your eye causes you to sin, pluck it out and cast it from you. It is better for you to enter into life with one eye, rather than having two eyes, to be cast into hell fire."

Jesus is not teaching that if we lust, for example, that we should literally pluck out one of our eyes, because even that would not keep us from lusting. What He is saying is that sin is serious, and it must be cut out of our lives at any cost. Why? Because the consequences of sin are eternal. If we willfully choose to sin, we will ultimately suffer eternal punishment in the Lake of Fire. Everyone in the world is accountable before God, because Romans 1 says that the heavens declare the glory of God. No one has an excuse for *not* coming to God, but those who have heard the teaching directly from God's Word will be judged even more strictly than those who have not.

In Matthew 18:10-11 Jesus says, "Take heed that you do not despise one of these little ones, for I say to you that in heaven their angels always see the face of My Father who is in heaven. For the Son of Man has come to save that which was lost." The main reason that Jesus Christ came to earth was to die the torturous death on the cross to save the lost. In light of Jesus' teaching, the importance of repentance is obviously vital to salvation.

The Robe of Righteousness

Jesus comes down hard on the church of Sardis because most of the church has slipped into Liberalism. They have made themselves an offense to the Gospel by rejecting the Deity of Jesus Christ and His atoning work on the cross. They have turned the truth of God into intellectualism. They have taken the foundational truths of the Word of God, and mixed them with secular humanism, resulting in the pollution of the minds of the students who have a true heart for God. Nevertheless, Jesus tells them in verse four that He knows His true followers. He promises to those who watch, and to those who remain clean from the stain of sin in their lives, a garment of righteousness. The life of a Christian is *not* a life of ease. We are saved by the free gift of God's grace, but then God expects us to live in His righteousness, and not to go back into our old ways of sin. We are commanded to walk *with* God, and only then are we counted worthy by God to inherit eternal life.

He who overcomes shall be clothed in white garments, and I will not blot out his name from the Book of Life; but I will confess his name before My Father and before His angels. The color white speaks of righteousness. Our righteousness can only come by putting our faith and trust in Jesus Christ. There is no way that we can earn righteousness on our own merit. When we come to

God through the righteousness of Jesus Christ, our name is written by God in the Book of Life. Jesus Christ will confess our name before God the Father, and before all of the angels in heaven. What a privilege! Notice how beautiful it is for those who choose to give their lives to Jesus Christ unreservedly.

Then the familiar challenge in verse six, **He who has an ear, let him hear what the Spirit says to the churches.** I hope that you do not hear anything that I say, but that you hear what the Holy Spirit is saying to you right now. What I say means nothing; it is only what God declares through His Holy Spirit that means anything.

I pray through this whole study of the seven churches of Revelation, that we will learn to submit our lives to Jesus Christ, and to repent, and get our lives right with God because He wants to do a mighty work in our lives.

SEVEN

THE LETTER TO THE CHURCH OF PHILADELPHIA

(Revelation 3:7-13)

"And to the angel of the church in Philadelphia write, 'These things says He who is holy, He who is true, He who has the key of David, He who opens and no one shuts, and shuts and no one opens: I know your works. See, I have set before you an open door, and no one can shut it; for you have a little strength, have kept My word, and have not denied My name. Indeed I will make those of the synagogue of Satan, who say they are Jews and are not, but lie–indeed I will make them come and worship before your feet, and to know that I have loved you. Because you have kept My command to persevere, I also will keep you from the hour of trial which shall come upon the whole world, to test those who dwell on the earth. Behold, I come quickly! Hold fast what you have, that no one may take your crown. He who overcomes, I will make him a pillar in the temple of My God, and he shall go out no more. And I will write on him the name of My God and the name of the city of My God, the New

Jerusalem, which comes down out of heaven from My God. And I will write on him My new name. He who has an ear, let him hear what the Spirit says to the churches.' "

The name Philadelphia means "city of brotherly love." The church of Philadelphia was not a powerful church, but they did have a little bit of strength. The church of Philadelphia is the remnant church, alive today, and will be gathered to Jesus Christ in the rapture. Hopefully, we are part of this church today.

By the world's standards, this church is weak: little strength, little influence, little in size. Its spiritual power, however, is mighty in witness. There is no rebuke from the Lord to this church; only praise. The church of Philadelphia is a revival church, its foundation built on glorious evangelical revival, and its vision focused on taking the Gospel of Christ to the whole world. Not only does this church stand blameless before man, it possesses profound spiritual blessings that only come from the holiness of God.

This letter to the church of Philadelphia verifies the fact that God's people will not be on earth during the Great Tribulation; it is the church that Jesus Christ has chosen to take out of the world. **Because you have kept My command to persevere, I also will keep you from the hour of trial which shall come upon the whole world, to test those who dwell on the earth.** The word *trial* also means "temptation, tribulation, or trouble," and refers to the Great

Tribulation. The Old Testament refers to this period as *the time of Jacob's trouble* (Jeremiah 30:7), or *the seventieth week of Daniel* (Daniel 9:27). The world has not yet experienced this hour of trial, but we can see from this passage, along with many others in the Bible, that those who are truly walking with Jesus Christ will be spared the final seven years on earth known as the Great Tribulation.

Once the church of Jesus Christ is taken out of the world, then the restraining power of the Holy Spirit will be removed, and the man of perdition, or the Antichrist, will rise to prominence to take control of the world. During the first half of the final seven-year period, this man of perdition will single-handedly regenerate economic and political stability in the world. His public relations campaign will be magnificent, and the entire world will embrace him as its savior. He will bring about peace and prosperity for three-and-a-half years. There will be a universal delusion of euphoria, until everything suddenly crumbles. "For when they say, 'Peace and safety!' then sudden destruction comes upon them, as labor pains upon a pregnant woman. And they shall not escape" (1 Thessalonians 5:3). The Antichrist will enter into the future Jewish temple which will be rebuilt in Jerusalem, and proclaim himself to be God. He will demand worship from everyone on earth, and those who refuse him will be executed (2 Thessalonians 2; Matthew 24:15).

At that point, God will begin to stir up the nation of Israel, and the Jews will finally recognize that Jesus Christ is their true Messiah. In order to escape the great persecution of the Antichrist, the Jews in Israel will flee to a city called Petra, located in Jordan, which is completely formed out of rock. There are cavernous rooms in this rock that can accommodate as many as ten thousand people. The only entrance to the city is through a narrow passageway in the rock accessible by foot or pack animal only. As the Jews flee Jerusalem to Petra, the Antichrist will send his armies to pursue them, just as Pharaoh did to Moses and the children of Israel.

God is Faithful to His Promises

The book of Genesis offers some fascinating insights into the ultimate destiny of the nation of Israel. In Genesis 12, God promises to make Abraham a great nation. The promise not only entails that his descendants would be numbered as the dust of the earth (Genesis 13:16), and as the stars of the heavens (Genesis 15:5), but that through his descendants, all the nations of the world would be blessed (Genesis 12:3). Most significant is the fact that the covenant will last forever (Genesis 17:13). Through this covenant with Abraham, God planned to redeem the entire human race. Jesus Christ is the fulfillment of that covenant. Jesus Christ came into the world from the seed of Abraham, and through Him, any man can be saved from the bondage of sin and death.

Genesis 22 narrates one of the most touching stories ever told. Abraham had been obedient to God throughout his entire life. God had promised Abraham that his descendants would be a great nation, but there was one minor problem: Abraham and Sarah had no children. Abraham, at this point, is over one hundred years-old, and Sarah is over ninety years-old, obviously well past the normal child-bearing age. The task, however, does not seem difficult to God, and subsequently, Sarah gives birth to their only son Isaac.

Then one day, several years later, God gives Abraham a rather unusual command (Genesis 22:2): Abraham is to take his only son Isaac, whom he loves dearly, and through whom God would fulfill His everlasting covenant, to the top of Mount Moriah, cut open his throat with a knife, and burn his body upon an altar. In Genesis 22:7 Isaac questions his father regarding the sacrificial lamb for the burnt offering. Abraham replies, "My son, God will provide for Himself the lamb for a burnt offering."

When they reach the top of the mountain, Abraham builds an altar, then binds Isaac to be slain. It is important to point out that Abraham is around one hundred thirty years-old, and Isaac around thirty years-old at this time, indicating complete and total obedience and submission by Isaac to his father, as well as by Abraham to God. Both acts of obedience establish the fact that Abraham and Isaac trust God implicitly. Abraham's reply that God would provide Himself a lamb for the offering is an incredible Messianic prophecy fulfilled in His Son Jesus Christ two thousand years later on that same mountain as He was slain for the sins of the world. By personally accepting the one supreme sacrifice of Jesus Christ, anyone can come to know God.

Satan the Destroyer

Ever since he was cast out of heaven, Satan's goal, has been to destroy the human race, harboring extra hatred for the church of Jesus Christ as it brings the good news of salvation to the world, and for Israel, God's chosen people through whom the Messiah came into the world to bring that salvation. Today, the Jews continually remind the world of the Holocaust of World War II when Hitler slaughtered six million Jews. The Bible, however, says that there will come a time during the Great Tribulation when even more Jews will be killed by the Antichrist than were killed by Hitler's Third Reich.

Revelation 12 foretells a conflict between a beast and a woman who bears a child. The woman represents the nation of Israel, and the beast represents the Antichrist who is governed and empowered by Satan. The prophet Zechariah predicts that as the Antichrist pursues the Jewish nation, he will annihilate two-thirds of them, and only by the grace of God, one-third will be preserved. God will then shelter that remnant in the city of Petra for the final forty-two months of the Great Tribulation. If God would not miraculously intervene, there would not be a single Jew left alive when He comes back to set up His kingdom on earth. God has always been faithful to the promise that He gave to Abraham. Even though the Jews have been scattered all over the world throughout history, they have managed to keep their Jewish identity and culture. God has always maintained a remnant of the Jewish nation unto Himself, because God is true to His Word.

Historical Background

The city of Philadelphia was located in what is now Asiatic Turkey, and was founded by Eumenes, the king of Pergamum, sometime during the second century B.C. Eumenes named the city after his brother Attalus who was nicknamed Philadelphus because of his fierce loyalty. Philadelphia's fertile land brought it much commercial prosperity, but it was often shaken by earthquakes, just like the state of California today. After repeated shakings, the city was finally destroyed by a massive earthquake in A.D. 17, along with the city of Sardis, and ten other cities in the Lydian valley. Today, the city of Philadelphia is called Alasehir, or the city of God.

As a period in church history, the church of Philadelphia was established around 1520 with the beginning of the Reformation, and will remain on earth until it is removed at the rapture of the church. During the Reformation this beautiful church was granted the open door which no one can shut—the door of missions to the world. The Gospel of Jesus Christ was carried to Africa, Asia, Europe, North America, and South America. God has opened doors for this church, and no one, aside from God Himself, can shut them.

Uncompromising Commitment to Christ

In verse 7 Jesus is presented **He who is holy, He who is true, He who has the key of David, He who opens and no one shuts, and shuts and no one opens.** Jesus Christ is represented in all of His sovereignty as a God of holiness; a God who gives Himself to His people. In turn, He requires His people to conform to His holy standard, and to separate themselves from the world.

Jesus Christ has the key of David. This is a fulfillment of Isaiah 22:22, "The key of the house of David I will lay on his shoulder; so he shall open, and no one shall shut; and he shall shut, and no one shall open." God has promised a beautiful relationship to those who answer His call. Those in the church of Philadelphia have seen the power of

God in their lives. They have been faithful to God's call. These people will not bow their knee to Satan. They will not sell out for the riches of this world, for the cheapness and the corruption of material goods. They have esteemed highly the great value of the kingdom of God.

Many in the church today are completely infatuated with the carnality of the world. Their fleshly appetite for the cheap and temporal pleasures utterly destroys any true spiritual growth in their lives, and thereby creates nothing but a nominal Christian lifestyle. They have no spiritual power, only useless religion. People struggle with their flesh because they do not read their Bibles regularly; they rarely, if ever, pray; they generally do not associate with any mature Christians. Their individual experiences validate what they consider to be Christianity. They follow Jesus Christ on their own terms. They straddle the fence between true Christianity and hedonism. They feel that they know Jesus as Savior, but He is certainly not the Lord of their lives.

There is a radical difference between professing Jesus Christ as Savior, and professing Him as Lord. The word *Lord* indicates supreme authority, controller, owner, or sovereign master. When Jesus Christ becomes the Lord of our lives, our relationship with Him becomes that of a slave to his master. We become the exclusive property of Jesus Christ. We are obligated to obey His every command. We no longer dictate the direction and activities of our own lives, but instead, constantly seek to please our Lord. If we decide what we will and will not do in our lives, Jesus Christ is not our Lord. In Luke 6:46 Jesus asked, "But why do you call Me 'Lord, Lord,' and do not do the things which I say?" If Jesus Christ is not our Lord, then neither is He our Savior. The believers who belong to the church of Philadelphia, apart from all others, know Jesus Christ as Lord of their lives.

Know Them by Their Fruits

Matthew 7 records the final portion of Jesus' Sermon on the Mount. In verse 15, Jesus warns us of false prophets within the church. There are people in the church who claim to be Christians, but they really are not. He goes on to explain in verses 16-20 that no matter what a person says about his faith, the only reliable indicator of what that person believes, is how he lives his life. Jesus summarizes the principle in verse 20, "Therefore by their fruits you will know them."

In verse 21, Jesus makes the distinction between a false and true profession, "Not everyone who says to Me, 'Lord, Lord,' shall enter the kingdom of heaven, but he who does the will of My Father in heaven." Only those who do God's will are God's children, and only they will enter the kingdom of heaven. Not everyone who claims that Jesus is his Lord will enter the kingdom of heaven. In verse 22, Jesus informs us that not just a few, but many people will be shocked on the Day of Judgment to discover that they have been condemned to eternal punishment because they did not practice the will of God during their lifetimes, "Many will say to Me in that day, 'Lord, Lord, have we not prophesied in Your name, cast out demons in Your name, and done many wonders in Your name?' " Notice how their lives were full of what they considered to be good works. They had works: prophecy, exorcism, and miracles. This was their confession to God. Jesus will respond, "And then I will declare to them, 'I never knew you; depart from Me, you who practice lawlessness!' " The problem is that they thought they knew Him, but He did not know them. We need to be careful that when we build a foundation, it is built upon the holiness of God. If it is not, then when it is tested, it will collapse.

A Solid Foundation

"Therefore whoever hears these sayings of Mine, and does them, I will liken him to a wise man who built his house on the rock: and the rain descended, the floods came, and the winds blew and beat on that house; and it did not fall, for it was founded on the rock. Now everyone who hears these sayings of Mine, and does not do them, will be like a foolish man who built his house on the sand: and the rain descended, the floods came, and the winds blew and beat on that house; and it fell. And great was its fall" (Matthew 7:24-27). The foundation of our lives must be built upon the rock of both hearing and doing the Word of God. Who is the Rock? The Rock is Jesus Christ. What are the rains, the floods, and the winds that beat upon the house? They are every trial and temptation that we go through in this life. If you find that you cannot sustain yourself as you go through trials and tribulations, and that you cannot overcome the temptations in your life, then this is evidence that you have built your house upon the sand, and not upon the Rock—Jesus Christ.

The man who builds his house on the Rock is the one who knows God and obeys His voice. The one who hears the Word of God, but does not obey it, is foolish. He is the one who builds his house on the sand. When the rains descend, the floods come, and the winds beat upon his house; it is completely destroyed. When the trials and tribulations come, this person falls into sin. He may have the outward appearance of good spiritual health, but when trouble comes into his life, rather than relying on the Lord, he resorts to the wisdom of the world to get himself out of trouble. His walk with the Lord gradually diminishes as the concealed sin in his life chokes out his fellowship with God. His life spirals rapidly downward. Sin begets worse sin, and his life is further and further distanced from the ways of the Lord, until eventually he is in worse condition than before he ever came to Jesus Christ.

The Cost of Discipleship

Throughout the gospels, Jesus taught that if anyone followed Him, he should first count the cost of discipleship. In Matthew 16:24 Jesus exhorts his disciples, "If anyone desires to come after Me, let him deny himself, and take up his cross, and follow Me." Although Jesus' exhortation is indeed one of beauty, most Christians have heard it so often that the sharpness of its meaning has faded somewhat. A closer inspection reveals the true impact.

The word *deny* means "to forget about yourself; emptying yourself from everything you possess." To take up your cross is not merely draping a piece of jewelry around your neck. The cross is an instrument of death—slow, agonizing, torturous death. To take up your cross is to die to yourself. When you become a Christian, your own desires are gradually eliminated as you take on the desires of our Lord Jesus Christ. Loosely paraphrased, Jesus is saying, "If you want to be My disciple, then empty yourself. Give up everything you own and everyone you love, and follow me to death." The decision to follow Jesus should not be made lightly. The cost of following Jesus Christ is God's holiness. Only if you honestly deny yourself and take up the cross, can you truly follow Him.

Jesus brings out another aspect of discipleship in verse 25, "For whoever desires to save his life will lose it, and whoever loses his life for My sake will find it." If you are not willing to give up your present life in this world, and your main priorities are the pleasures of this world, then you will ultimately be left with nothing. Those who are into promiscuous lifestyles, whose gods are sex, drugs, and rock and roll, may appear to be having fun right now, and they may even have themselves convinced that they are experiencing life to its fullest, but when they come to the end of their lives, a point which all of us come to sooner or later, they will find themselves in misery. Jesus Christ conveys no ambiguity in this message.

In verse 26, Jesus asks, "For what is a man profited if he gains the whole world, and loses his own soul? Or what will a man give in exchange for his soul?" What can you possibly gain in this world that will make up for losing your soul? What will you pay to gain entrance into the kingdom of God? What are the pleasures of this world worth from an eternal perspective? What is the price of your eternal soul? For what are you willing to sell out? Judas Iscariot sold Jesus Christ to be crucified for thirty pieces of silver. In Mark 14:21 Jesus says that it would have been better for Judas never to have been born. God allows each one of us to make that eternal choice. Unfortunately, many people sell out cheaply.

God, however, did not pay a cheap price for salvation,

"For God so loved the world that He gave His only begotten Son, that whoever believes in Him should not perish but have everlasting life." Jesus Christ left the glory of His heavenly dwelling place to come to earth and suffer the excruciating death on the cross for all of us. On the third day, He resurrected from the grave. When He ascended to heaven to sit at the right hand of God the Father in eternal glory, He imparted to us His Holy Spirit and the power of His resurrection. All He asks of us in return is unconditional surrender here and now. If we are willing to give up our will to His, He is anxiously waiting to bestow upon us eternal blessings beyond our comprehension. The price of eternal life is complete submission to Him. As we begin to submit our lives to God, He begins to empower us for His service. The more we die to ourselves, the more like Him we become. As with any experience though, we cannot properly discern the benefits until after we have elected to pay the price. We must count the cost.

Doers of the Word, Not Just Hearers

Matthew 19:16 gives the account of a rich young ruler who came to Jesus with the hope of finding an easy way to eternal security. Jesus perceived that the greatest priority in this man's life was his money, so He told him to go and sell all that he had, give it to the poor, and come and follow Him. The rich man departed in sadness because he realized that he could not afford to pay the price. What is the most important thing in your life? Is it Jesus, or something keeping you from following Jesus?

Jesus Christ is the living God, and He is holy. He is our eternal security. He is always there when we need

Him. Because we need Him, we must commit our entire lives to Him. God's love and grace and mercy cannot be used like a credit card. Every one of us deserves to be cast into the Lake of Fire for eternity, but through the sacrifice of Jesus Christ, we have been given the opportunity of eternal life. To go back to our old lifestyles would be to commit spiritual suicide. We are accountable to God for the way we live our lives.

Jesus consistently taught that merely hearing His Word is not sufficient. We must not only *hear* His word, we must *do* what He tells us to do. Many people hear many sermons. They are tuned into Christian radio stations all day, hearing one Bible study after another. They go to church and do everything they are supposed to do as religious people, but they are not really in tune with God. There are many people who seem to be good listeners, but they fail to do what they are commanded to do.

The Pharisees and the scribes of Jesus' day had the same problem. Jesus accused them of putting burdens on people that they themselves did not even carry. We need to be very careful with the Word of God. There is an eternal gap between believers and non-believers. Jesus reveals to us in Matthew 7:21 that people on both sides of the gap will profess Him as Lord. You can profess Jesus Christ all you want, but if you are not doing God's will, one day you will find yourself standing before the throne of the Almighty God, and hearing those words of rejection, "I never knew you; depart from Me, you who practice lawlessness!"

Faith Brings Strength

I know your works. See, I have set before you an

open door, and no one can shut it; for you have a little strength, have kept My word, and have not denied My name. Jesus knows our works. He is fully aware of everything that we have ever done or thought. He has set before us an open door. The door of opportunity is wide open to share the Gospel of Jesus Christ with a dying world. If we use our talents and abilities for God's glory, then He will bless and cultivate them.

Conversely, if we use our talents and abilities for ourselves, then we will reap what we have sown. God has given us an open door, and no one can shut it. Why? Because we have kept His Word, and have not denied His name. What a beautiful promise.

The church that will be taken in the rapture is not a super-church. It will have a little strength, but it will have kept God's Word, and will not have denied His name. These are the believers who hear the Word of God, and their lives are changed. Their confession of Jesus Christ is manifested by their lives to everyone around them. In Matthew 10:32-33, Jesus promises us, "Therefore whoever confesses Me before men, him I will also confess before My Father who is in heaven. But whoever denies Me before men, him I will also deny before My Father who is in heaven." We must understand who we are in Jesus Christ. The all-important aspect of our lives is not what we can do for God, but what God already has done for us. When we gain an understanding of what God has done for us, then we can begin to seek what He can do through us.

In Romans 12:1-2, the Apostle Paul informs us of God's desire for our lives: "I beseech you therefore, brethren, by the mercies of God, that you present your bodies a living sacrifice, holy, acceptable to God, which is your reasonable service. And do not be conformed to this world, but be transformed by the renewing of your mind, that you may prove what is that good and acceptable and perfect will of God." God wants us to submit our bodies entirely to His service: our ears, our eyes, our mouth, our hands, our feet. When we can say to Him, "Here I am, Lord, do with my life as you see fit," then God can use us. The experience of being used by God naturally transforms us into the image of God. We will never be the same again.

Representatives of Christ

Jesus promises in verse 9, **Indeed I will make those of the synagogue of Satan, who say they are Jews and are not, but lie–indeed I will make them come and worship before your feet, and to know that I have loved you.** He is referring to the Jews who had denied Jesus Christ. A Jew, in the true spiritual sense, is a child of God. He is one who participates in God's eternal covenant with Abraham. To deny Jesus Christ is to deny that covenant, and thus discard the eternal heritage of the Jew.

The Pharisees mistakenly assumed that their blood relationship to Abraham guaranteed them favor in the sight of God, but John the Baptist informed them otherwise in Matthew 3:9, "Do not think to say to yourselves, 'We have Abraham as our father.' For I say to you that God is able to raise up children to Abraham from these stones. And even now the ax is laid to the root of the trees. Therefore every tree which does not bear good fruit is cut down and thrown into the fire." Jesus' statement to the church of Philadelphia affirmed the fact that those who had denied Him as their Messiah were not true Jews, but they had made themselves part of the synagogue of Satan.

The modern-day church is full of people who claim to be Christians, but worship a Christ of their own fabrication. They attend church regularly, and speak fluent Christian jargon, but they are not authentic Christians. By their lifestyles they deny the name of Jesus Christ on a regular basis. Christians are representatives of Jesus Christ. We either represent Him accurately or inaccurately. Moses, for example, misrepresented God when he smote the rock twice, rather than speaking to the rock as he had been instructed by God. So often, Christians represent Jesus Christ as a drunkard, or drug user, or fornicator, or adulterer, or liar. Bumper stickers and Jesus T-shirts are not the qualifications of a Christian. Our lives reveal what we believe in the depths of our hearts—whether we live for ourselves, or for Jesus Christ.

Those involved in Christian ministry are especially conspicuous. If we profess the name of Jesus Christ, people will be watching us when we least expect it. Most people, at least in the United States, have heard the name of Jesus, but when they observe the lives of Christians, they often *hear* one message, and *see* a completely different one. When we meet someone who is honestly seeking Jesus Christ, our behavior can either lead them to Christ, or drive them away from Him for all eternity. We are all accountable to the truth that God has given us.

Obedience Brings Preservation

Because you have kept My command to persevere, I also will keep you from the hour of trial which shall come upon the whole world, to test those who dwell on

the earth. True believers are not going to be here during the Great Tribulation because the true church of Jesus Christ will be raptured out of this world before God's wrath is poured out.

Throughout man's history on this planet, God has always spared His people from the outpouring of His wrath on the earth. The book of Genesis records how God saved Enoch from the wrath of the coming flood by translating him to heaven without physical death. We also have been given the examples of Noah in the ark during the great flood, Lot being escorted from Sodom and Gomorrah by angels before God caused fire to rain down, and the passing over of the angel of death with the children of Israel during their Egyptian captivity. That is the hope we have in Christ. Second Timothy 1:12 says, "I know whom I have believed and am persuaded that He is able to keep what I have committed to Him until that Day."

The precise timing of the rapture is certainly not worth arguing. The way that we live our lives is all that counts. If we are not living for Jesus Christ, then we will certainly encounter tough times. If we cannot live for Him now, it is doubtful that we will be able to die for Him when all hell breaks loose on earth in the near future. Count the cost. Jesus Christ is coming soon for the church of Philadelphia. We need to be ready. We have His promise of protection.

Great Rewards for the Faithful

Behold, I come quickly! Hold fast what you have, that no one may take your crown. In other words, "Hold on!" We are not to be discouraged. We are not to allow Satan to lure us into some sin that will disqualify us from serving Jesus Christ. We are to hold on to the Word of Truth.

He who overcomes, I will make him a pillar in the temple of My God, and he shall go out no more. And I will write on him the name of My God and the name of the city of My God, the New Jerusalem, which comes down out of heaven from My God. And I will write on him My new name. Here is eternal security–overcoming the power of sin in our lives through faith in the shed blood of Jesus Christ.

He who has an ear, let him hear what the Spirit says to the churches. To whom is the Spirit speaking? He is speaking to the churches. Who are the churches? You and I are the church. God has given us so much, and He expects a return on His investment. Through His love, grace, and mercy, He has given us the potential of storing for ourselves eternal treasures in heaven.

EIGHT

THE LETTER TO THE CHURCH OF LAODICEA

(Revelation 3:14-22)

"And to the angel of the church of the Laodiceans write, 'These things says the Amen, the Faithful and True Witness, the Beginning of the creation of God: I know your works, that you are neither cold nor hot. I could wish you were cold or hot. So then, because you are lukewarm, and neither cold nor hot, I will spew you out of My mouth. Because you say, "I am rich, have become wealthy, and have need of nothing"–and do not know that you are wretched, miserable, poor, blind, and naked–I counsel you to buy from Me gold refined in the fire, that you may be rich; and white garments, that you may be clothed, that the shame of your nakedness may not be revealed; and anoint your eyes with eye salve, that you may see. As many as I love, I rebuke and chasten. Therefore be zealous and repent. Behold, I stand at the door and knock. If anyone hears My voice and opens the door, I will come in to him and dine with him, and he with Me. To him who overcomes I will grant to sit with Me on My throne, as I also overcame and sat down with My Father on His throne. He who has an ear, let him hear what the Spirit says to the churches.' "

-8-

The historical perspective of the church of Laodicea is very important. This church is called the "apostate" church. It began around 1900, and along with its predecessors, Thyatira and Sardis, it will continue through the Great Tribulation. The people in the church of Laodicea are going to be under heavy pressure to take the mark of the beast from the Antichrist which will allow them to do business in a global society, economic system, and government. A one-world economic system will implement some type of identification mark on either the forehead or the right hand of every man, woman, and child on earth. No one will be able to buy or sell or do any type of business transaction without this mark. Revelation 13:16-18 describes the mark of the beast: "He causes all, both small and great, rich and poor, free and slave, to receive a mark on their right hand or on their foreheads, and that no one may buy or sell except one who has the mark or the name of the beast, or the number of his name. Here is wisdom. Let him who has understanding calculate the number of the beast, for it is the number of a man: His number is 666."

Over the past several years, many people, including Hollywood producers, have tried to identify the meaning of this mark, but we may not know its full ramifications until it is actually in place. The technology presently exists, though, to embed a microchip under the skin's surface which could contain a person's entire history and credit record, allowing for business transactions without cash, credit cards, or external identification. There would seem to be a great advantage to this type of common, unified, cashless society. The absence of cash would eliminate much red tape in world trade, as well as eliminating a large portion of crime in the world. For reasons not completely understood by man at this time, however, the Bible warns that anyone who takes this mark will be damned to the Lake of Fire for all eternity. Being killed by the Antichrist will be infinitely better than submitting to his mark. Revelation 14:11 describes the consequences of taking the mark of the beast: "And the smoke of their torment ascends forever and ever; and they have no rest day or night, who worship the beast and his image, and whoever receives the mark of his name."

We have been moving toward a cashless, global society for at least the last three decades. We are living on borrowed time. No one can tell us precisely when Jesus Christ will return to this earth, but many biblical prophecies have been fulfilled over the past twenty years that would indicate that His return is soon. God puts that hope in our hearts. The first century believers were convinced that Jesus Christ would return during their lifetimes but He has not returned yet. Perhaps it was God's intention for Christians in every age to believe that Jesus was coming back in their lifetimes so that they would always be ready for Him. Our anticipation of Christ's return provides us with a great hope, because God Himself has given us His promise. We are beginning to see God's promises coming to pass in this age.

Historical Background

The ancient city of Laodicea was a very wealthy inland city on the banks of the Lycus River, about forty miles southeast of Philadelphia, ninety miles due east of Ephesus, and only about ten miles west of old Colosse. It had a population of about seventeen thousand, most of whom were wealthy, socially prominent citizens who raised sheep that produced a fine, soft, glossy black wool used in the manufacturing of expensive, designer label clothing and rugs. As a result, Laodicea served as an important commercial center at a major crossroads in this part of the Roman Empire. Laodicea was also noted throughout the Roman world for its highly-esteemed medical school. The Laodicean physicians had developed a salve that was known to heal a wide variety of eye infections. The people of Laodicea were contented with their lives. They had more than enough wealth and material comforts than they needed, and they had a vision for the future success of their textile and medical industries. How ironic that in verse 17, Jesus diagnoses their condition as being wretched, miserable, poor, blind, and naked!

Although the city of Laodicea had many natural advantages, it had one serious shortcoming–a lack of good drinking water. Nearly all the streams in the area came from hot springs filled with impurities, thus, the reference to the Laodicean church in verse 16 as being "lukewarm, and neither cold nor hot." Archaeological excavations at Laodicea have revealed that the city apparently had tried to solve its water supply problem by bringing in water from an outside source through stone pipes. The pipes they used, however, contained limestone deposits.

Consequently, the water that was piped in was not much better than the old supply from the hot springs. This serious water problem may have led to Laodicea's eventual decline. The Apostle Paul evidently wrote a letter to the Laodiceans, as referred to in Colossians 4:16, but it apparently has been lost.

Laodicea was probably one of the wealthiest cities during the first century, and the church adjusted itself to that high lifestyle. The church of Laodicea in church history will be similarly infatuated with worldly wealth. The first 3-1/2 years of the Great Tribulation will be a time of tremendous prosperity in the world, and consequently, the church will benefit financially. True spiritual understanding will be replaced with an intensely materialistic religion. The name Laodicea means "judgment of the people." God will, in fact, judge the people of this church during the second half of the Great Tribulation.

A Lukewarm Church

And to the angel of the church of the Laodiceans write, "These things says the Amen, the Faithful and True Witness, the Beginning of the creation of God." The New King James Version says, "the Beginning of the creation of God," but a literal translation of the Greek would read, "in the Beginning of creation of God." This is in reference to Jesus Christ. The characteristics illustrated are the faithfulness and truth of Jesus Christ because He created all things in the beginning. Jesus Himself is the faithful Witness of the condition of the church. The people themselves had no witness. Despite the fact that they received the personal witness of the living God, Jesus Christ

Himself, they completely missed the point that *He* is all they need, not the church, not themselves, not the riches of the world. Jesus Christ is God. There is no One else but Him. He is the only One upon whom we can depend.

There is no commendation to the church of Laodicea. Verses 15 and 16 clearly communicate Jesus' displeasure: **I know your works, that you are neither cold nor hot. I could wish you were cold or hot. So then, because you are lukewarm, and neither cold nor hot, I will spew you out of My mouth.** This rebuke is directed at their moral and spiritual condition and lifestyle. These people were spiritually dead, and yet they thought their lives were right on target with God.

A modern-day example of this mindset can be found in people who regularly attend church. They hear the pastor's message, even following along in their Bibles. By all appearances, while they are in church, they are Christians, but when they leave church, there is no conviction in their lives. The Word of God brings about no change in character, lifestyle, or habit. To them, the Bible is merely a collection of nice words. These people work hard to prevent, ignore, or deny the Holy Spirit from working in their lives. They are spiritually dead.

The church of Laodicea is the last, and by far, the most pitiful of the seven churches. They are in terrible condition. It would be better to be a heathen than to be a member of this church. Our Lord compares this church to the nauseating sensation of a lukewarm drink. Imagine pouring a cup of coffee, thinking that it was going to be piping hot, but bringing it to your lips and taking a sip, you find it is only lukewarm. Or imagine after a grueling physical workout, searching desperately for a cold drink, and finally spotting a soda machine in the corner of the gym. In great anticipation you pop open a can and take a hearty swig, only to discover that the soda is lukewarm. That same feeling and taste perfectly illustrate the word *disgusting*.

A lukewarm Christian is one who is neither on fire or zealous for Jesus Christ, nor a non-believer. He is one who plays both sides of the net, according to personal convenience and gain. He could never see himself in the world living and practicing overt sin, but at the same time he is unwilling to allow the Holy Spirit to make any deep and lasting changes in his lifestyle or character. There is no burning desire to grow closer and closer to the Lord, to become more like Him, especially if it means making personal sacrifice.

A Perfect Illustration

Jesus provides an excellent illustration of the widely varying conditions of the human heart in the parable He gives in Matthew 13:1-9, "On the same day Jesus went out of the house and sat by the sea. And great multitudes were gathered together to Him, so that He got into a boat and sat; and the whole multitude stood on the shore. Then He spoke many things to them in parables, saying: 'Behold, a sower went out to sow. And as he sowed, some seed fell by the wayside; and the birds came and devoured them. Some fell on stony places, where they did not have much earth; and they immediately sprang up because they had no depth of earth. But when the sun was up they were scorched, and because they had no root they withered away. And some fell among thorns, and the thorns sprang up and choked them. But others fell on good ground and yielded a crop: some a hundredfold, some sixty, some thirty. He who has ears to hear, let him hear!' " Jesus often used parables, or storytelling, to illustrate important truths of life.

In Matthew 13:18-23, He gives us the correct interpretation: "Therefore hear the parable of the sower: When anyone hears the word of the kingdom, and does not understand it, then the wicked one comes and snatches away what was sown in his heart. This is he who received seed by the wayside." This type of person sits down to listen to the message, hears the Word of God, is impressed with what he has heard, but the moment he walks out of church, he forgets everything. The enemy, Satan, plucks away the seed of the Word of God. This person lacks faith in God, so the Word of God cannot grow in his heart.

"But he who received the seed on stony places, this is he who hears the word and immediately receives it with joy; yet he has no root in himself, but endures only for a while. For when tribulation or persecution arises because of the word, immediately he stumbles" (Matthew 13:20-21). This type of person hears the Word of God and is immediately convicted of his sin. He is impressed with the message of the Gospel, feels the need for God in his life, and responds to His call. He accepts Jesus Christ as his personal Savior, gets a Bible, and reads it diligently for a month or so. Suddenly, trouble finds its way into his life, and his commitment to Jesus Christ quickly dissolves. There is no depth to his conviction because his commitment is purely an emotional response. His life is dictated by his emotions, and he has no spiritual roots.

"Now he who received seed among the thorns is he who hears the word, and the cares of this world and the deceitfulness of riches choke the word, and he becomes unfruitful" (Matthew 13:22). This is the lukewarm Christian. Because of the cares of this world, and the deceitfulness of riches, his faith is choked out, and he becomes unfruitful. He has never truly known the full power of Jesus Christ by completely surrendering to Him. He considers Christ his Savior, but he has not made Him his Lord. It is one of the most dangerous places that a person can be spiritually because he has attempted to fool God, but has only fooled himself. He is completely blind to his own hypocrisy.

"But he who received seed on the good ground is he who hears the word and understands it, who indeed bears fruit and produces: some a hundredfold, some sixty, some thirty" (Matthew 13:23). A true Christian bears lasting fruit in his life. This is evidence of his commitment to Christ. That commitment to Christ usually separates him from the world, as well as from uncommitted Christians. To profess Jesus Christ as Lord, and to live for Him are two entirely different things.

Give yourself a little test right now. On a scale from one to ten—one being the most evil, rebellious person on the face of the earth, the person who absolutely hates God, and ten being the most mature Christian in the world, the person who is simply on fire for Jesus Christ, and whose life bears abundant fruit. The church of Laodicea is at the number five spot—lukewarm. Numbers one through four are frigid, cold, chilly, and cool. Numbers six through ten are warm, comfortable, hot, and on fire. This scale gauges desire, not maturity; availability, not ability. Where do you fit?

Millions of people all over the world regularly attend

Bible-teaching churches. How many of them truly know Jesus Christ as Lord? How many people are actually going to be taken up in the rapture of the church? If Jesus Christ was to come back tonight, how many people can say right now that they would be ready? Do you know for certain that you will be with Him? Is there any doubt in your mind? The Apostle Paul exhorts us in 2 Corinthians 13:5, "Examine yourselves as to whether you are in the faith. Prove yourselves." Ask yourself the questions, "Do I have any fruit in my life? Is there any evidence in my life, other than the fact that I go to church, that I am a Christian?"

If you are cold, then you will know it, and if you are hot, you will know it as well. If you are lukewarm, though, the whole issue will be foggy. The condition of the lukewarm Christian is a lack of desire to read the Bible, to pray, or to go to church. There is no hunger and thirst for God in his life. He does not have the joy of the Lord. His spiritual condition is pathetic in the eyes of God. Jesus said he will spew that person out of His mouth.

Deceived

The word *spew*, softened a bit by the King James translators, literally means "to vomit." To be vomited from the mouth of Jesus Christ means to be utterly rejected. The lukewarm Christian will not enter the kingdom of God. This is certainly not a desirable response from our Creator on the day of His holy and righteous judgment. Unfortunately, though, this is the church that is developing quickly in these last days before Christ's return.

There are church goers today who are completely deceiving themselves in their liberal and worldly thoughts.

Some of them do not believe that Jesus Christ is God. Some believe they can teach and practice any manner of false doctrine. Some believe they can drink, do drugs, or live in sexual sin. All of them believe that God will accept them into His kingdom without any such radical measure as repentance in their lives. They ignore the conviction of the Holy Spirit in their hearts, if their hearts have not already been seared. They have attempted to cheapen God's grace, watering down the Gospel message of Jesus and resulting in a new gospel of their own creation (Galatians 1:6-12).

Paul warned the first century church of the same pitfall in 1 Corinthians 6:9-20:

> "Do you not know that the unrighteous will not inherit the kingdom of God? Do not be deceived. Neither fornicators, nor idolaters, nor adulterers, nor homosexuals, nor sodomites, nor thieves, nor covetous, nor drunkards, nor revilers, nor extortioners will inherit the kingdom of God. And such were some of you. But you were washed, but you were sanctified, but you were justified in the name of the Lord Jesus and by the Spirit of our God. All things are lawful for me, but all things are not helpful. All things are lawful for me, but I will not be brought under the power of any. Foods for the stomach and the stomach for foods, but God will destroy both it and them. Now the body is not for sexual immorality but for the Lord, and the Lord for the body. And God both raised up the Lord and will also raise us up by His power. Do you not know that your bodies are members of Christ? Shall I then take the members of Christ and make them members of a harlot? Certainly not! Or do you not know that he who is joined to a harlot is one body with her? For 'The two,' He says, 'shall become one flesh.' But he who

is joined to the Lord is one spirit with Him. Flee sexual immorality. Every sin that a man does is outside the body, but he who commits sexual immorality sins against his own body. Or do you not know that your body is the temple of the Holy Spirit who is in you, whom you have from God, and you are not your own? For you were bought at a price; therefore glorify God in your body and in your spirit, which are God's."

When a Christian sins and refuses to go to the cross of Jesus Christ right away, he is robbed of his spiritual peace, and the longer he stays away from the cross, the harder his heart becomes. After ignoring the conviction of the Holy Spirit for a long enough time, the heavens begin to sound like they are made of brass, as though God is not listening anymore. He begins to feel like he is all alone; that the anointing in his life is gone.

Although we must not always react to our feelings, they are often an indication that we know we are living in sin, and are refusing to repent of it. We isolate ourselves from the truth of Jesus Christ, and put ourselves in an extremely dangerous position. If we insist on living in that sinful state, we open the door for Satan to come in and wreak havoc in our lives. That is why Jesus Christ exhorts five of the seven churches to repent now and return wholly to Him.

Without Repentance

Because you say, 'I am rich, have become wealthy, and have need of nothing'–and do not know that you are wretched, miserable, poor, blind, and naked?– . . . . The Laodicean church was saying, "I don't need God. I have become wealthy. I don't need anything." It is always sad when man's dependence and trust is in himself or his fellowman, rather than in God. The people of the church of Laodicea are not willing to admit to their sins because their trust and dependence is on God's past mercies and past grace. They have, in their minds, arrived at such a high level of spiritual perfection that they resent anyone who would question their behavior, actions, or teachings. They quickly remind anyone who would, indeed, question them, that Christians are not to judge one another, and that God is forgiving, gentle, kind, merciful, and loving.

They ignore the full counsel of Scripture, however, when they overlook the fact the Christians are commanded to guard the truth entrusted to them, to be spiritually discerning of the teaching they hear, and to test the spirits of those doing the teaching to see if they be from God. They also conveniently put aside other facts about God and His character that are just as important, namely, that He is just, that He cannot lie, that His Word will never pass away, and that sin without repentance must be punished.

If we sin willfully with no true repentance, then there is no forgiveness for our sin (Hebrews 10:26-31; 1 John 1:6, 8, 2:4). We must deal with our sins. We must deal with our hearts. The Apostle Paul writes in Romans 1:18-19, "For the wrath of God is revealed from heaven against all ungodliness and unrighteousness of men, who suppress the truth in unrighteousness, because what may be known of God is manifest in them, for God has shown it to them." James 4:17 makes it even tougher, "Therefore, to him who knows to do good and does not do it, to him it is sin."

When a person has the Holy Spirit within him, he is perfectly aware of the difference between right and wrong.

If that person continues to do wrong, despite the conviction of the Holy Spirit, he is in for major problems. God will not tolerate willful sin. A person may think, like Samson, that he will stand up as he has in the past, and take care of the problems in his life, believing that God will be with him. As Samson discovered the hard way, however, when he stood up to take on the Philistines after Delilah cut his hair, the Spirit of the Lord had departed from him. God was no longer with him, and he was defeated. It is a fact that a person can presume the grace of God one too many times. We must be careful not to presume upon God's grace.

Not Everyone Will Make It

In Matthew 7:21 Jesus declares, "Not everyone who says to Me, 'Lord, Lord,' shall enter the kingdom of heaven, but he who does the will of My Father in heaven." The Apostle Paul echoes this truth in Galatians 5:16-21, "I say then: Walk in the Spirit, and you shall not fulfill the lust of the flesh. For the flesh lusts against the Spirit, and the Spirit against the flesh; and these are contrary to one another, so that you do not do the things that you wish. But if you are led by the Spirit, you are not under the law. Now the works of the flesh are evident, which are: adultery, fornication, uncleanness, licentiousness, idolatry, sorcery, hatred, contentions, jealousies, outbursts of wrath, selfish ambitions, dissensions, heresies, envy, murders, drunkenness, revelries, and the like; of which I tell you beforehand, just as I also told you in time past, that those who practice such things will not inherit the kingdom of God."

Keep in mind that Paul is addressing Christians in the

book of Galatians. The Spirit and the flesh are contrary to one another. We cannot do what pleases our own flesh, and also please the Spirit of God.

The passage in Galatians is not an isolated reference. Ephesians 5:1-7 says, "Therefore be followers of God as dear children. And walk in love, as Christ also has loved us and given Himself for us, an offering and a sacrifice to God for a sweet-smelling aroma. But fornication and all uncleanness or covetousness, let it not even be named a-mong you, as is fitting for saints; neither filthiness, nor foolish talking, nor coarse jesting, which are not fitting, but rather giving of thanks. For this you know, that no fornica-tor, unclean person, nor covetous man, who is an idolater, has any inheritance in the kingdom of Christ and God. Let no one deceive you with empty words, for because of these things the wrath of God comes upon the sons of disobedi-ence. Therefore do not be partakers with them." Notice again that Paul is writing to Christians.

If you are a child of God, and you are struggling with one of these sins, you need to earnestly pray that God will help you to remove it from your life. The bottom line, though, is that in order for God to cleanse us of any partic-ular sinful habit, we must *want* to be cleansed of it. We must acquire a hatred for our sins if we are to rid our lives of their influences. Just as a surgeon must cut out a malig-nant tumor from a patient's body in order to save his life, we must cut sin out of our lives. If we continually return to our sins, presuming that God will forgive us before we even do them, then the Bible says that we will have no in-heritance in the kingdom of God. God *will* pour out His wrath upon the sons of disobedience, so we are not to share in their rebellion against God.

God's Call Demands Holiness

I counsel you to buy from Me gold refined in the fire, that you may be rich; and white garments, that you may be clothed, that the shame of your nakedness may not be revealed; and anoint your eyes with eye salve, that you may see. Gold and white garments refer to God's righteousness; fire speaks of purification. God wants to give us salve for our eyes so that we can discern spiritual things. The people of the Laodicean church did not possess God's righteousness and purity because they had no spiritual discernment. They were ignorant of God's precepts because their eyes had been blinded by spiritual darkness.

As many as I love, I rebuke and chasten. Therefore be zealous and repent. When we have sin in our lives, God disciplines us because He loves us. Although the discipline sometimes seems to be tough, it serves to remove the sin from our lives that would lead us to eternal death. Our response should be zealous repentance. We must aggressively change the direction in which we are going. God wants us to turn and run from our sin. The entire twelfth chapter of Hebrews explains the principle of God's discipline for His children.

First Corinthians 11 records an instance in the early church that called for God's discipline. The people in the Corinthian church had turned their communion services into drunken orgies. The Apostle Paul revealed to them that because of their unconfessed sin, some of them had become weak, some had become sick, and some had even died. God may take what we would consider extreme measures in order to get us back into His fold. Often an extended hospital stay gets people's attention. If physical affliction will cause spiritual health, then the overall effect is good (1 Corinthians 5:1-5). God loves us, and He is willing to discipline us in order to teach us His ways. God may even take our lives if necessary because He sees our end results. We need to get our lives right with God.

An Open Invitation

Behold, I stand at the door and knock. If anyone hears My voice and opens the door, I will come in to him and dine with him, and he with Me. Where is Jesus Christ in the church of Laodicea? He is outside, patiently knocking at the door, waiting to be invited inside. He would like to come into our hearts, but He will not force His way in. We must invite Him. Jesus wants to have beautiful fellowship with us if we will only allow Him. Notice how much God wants to mend our relationship with Him. He does not want anyone to go to hell.

However, God has given us a free will. He will not force us to take the direction that He wants for us. He allows us to walk down the path toward death if we choose. He will chasten us if we are His children, but if we ignore the chastening, He will let us go the way that seems right to us. If we kick God out of our lives, He will leave. He will not force us to obey Him. He wants us to love Him out of our own free wills. He wants a love relationship, not a religious relationship.

As Jesus stands outside the door of our hearts, He knocks. If we open the door, and ask Him to come back inside our hearts, He steps inside and cleans up the messes that we have made of our lives, no matter what we have done in the past. He reestablishes fellowship with us, provides joy and peace in our hearts, blesses our lives, and begins to use us to spread His love to everyone around us.

What is the ultimate result of opening the door of your heart to Jesus Christ? **To him who overcomes I will grant to sit with Me on My throne, as I also overcame and sat down with My Father on His throne.** This promise is for those who overcome, not for those who are defeated by sin and temptation. Jesus Christ will return to earth with all of His saints, and He will reign as king over all of the inhabitants of the earth. Jesus Christ promises partnership with Him on His throne if we overcome this world and its temptations. He has given us His Spirit to do that, and He Himself promises, "In the world you will have tribulation; but be of good cheer, I have overcome the world."

Those who submit to the authority of Jesus Christ here on earth will be given authority to rule in heaven. As we prove to be faithful in the small things that God gives us here and now, He will give us increasing responsibilities in the life to come. The better we handle the responsibility that God gives us here on earth, the more responsibility we will be given when we get to heaven.

He who has an ear, let him hear what the Spirit says to the churches. The tireless Spirit of God still pleads with the hearts of individuals. Seven times He calls to those who have an ear. Do you have an ear to hear? Can you hear Him knocking? Procrastination is the same as rejection. Jesus says in Matthew 12:30, "He who is not with Me is against Me, and he who does not gather with Me scatters abroad." If you want to be with Jesus Christ eternally, you must abandon your sin, and come to Him now. This offer is for a limited time only! He is still outside knocking because He loves you so much. Open the door to your heart and invite Him in right now!

NINE

HOW TO BE BORN AGAIN

(John 3:16-18)

"For God so loved the world that He gave His only begotten Son, that whoever believes in Him should not perish but have everlasting life. For God did not send His Son into the world to condemn the world, but that the world through Him might be saved. He who believes in Him is not condemned; but he who does not believe is condemned already, because he has not believed in the name of the only begotten Son of God."

-9-

The Bible tells us in Romans 3:23 that "all have sinned and fall short of the glory of God." That means that no
matter how good or how bad a person may be, he is still a
sinner in the eyes of God. No amount of good works can
ever earn a person into heaven. In fact, that's what religion
has become over the last twenty centuries—man trying to
earn his way to God. God, however, is holy and cannot
even look upon sin.

The Bible also tells us in Hebrews 9:22 that "without
shedding of blood there is no remission" of sin. Beginning
with Genesis 3:21, through the entire Old Testament, we
see that God provided a system of sacrifice by which man
could shed the blood of an animal in order to have his sins
forgiven. The Old Testament sacrificial system, however,
only served as a covering for man's sin, not as a completed
redemption. The old sacrificial system, though, personally
illustrated the serious and far-reaching effects of sin, the
holiness of God, and man's hopelessness in his attempts to
live a sinless life. The old system, too, pointed to a future
time when God would provide Himself a perfect sacrifice,
offered once and for all for the sins of the world. That perfect sacrifice would be His Son, the God-Man Jesus Christ.

In John 1:29 John the Baptist says of Jesus, "Behold!
The Lamb of God who takes away the sin of the world!"

In John 3:16 Jesus Himself says, "For God so loved the world that He gave His only begotten Son, that whoever believes in Him should not perish but have everlasting life." In Romans 5:1-2 the Apostle Paul writes, "Therefore, having been justified by faith, we have peace with God through our Lord Jesus Christ, through whom also we have access by faith into this grace in which we stand, and rejoice in hope of the glory of God." In Hebrews 9:26 the writer writes that Jesus Christ "has appeared to put away sin by the sacrifice of Himself." In 1 Peter 1:18-19 the Apostle Peter writes, "Knowing that you were not redeemed with perishable things, like silver or gold, from your aimless conduct received by tradition from your fathers, but with the precious blood of Christ, as of a lamb without blemish and without spot."

Jesus, then, is the solution to man's sin problem. He has bridged the uncrossable gap between man and God with the cross on which He was crucified on Calvary. On that cross Jesus took the sins of the entire world, past, present, and future, upon Himself. The Bible tells us in Romans 5:8 that "God demonstrates His own love toward us, in that while we were still sinners, Christ died for us." In 1 Timothy 1:15 Paul writes, "This is a faithful saying and worthy of all acceptance, that Christ Jesus came into the world to save sinners . . . ."

Jesus Christ, through His death and resurrection, makes it possible for man to approach God the Father, but only those who receive Him by faith will actually inherit the kingdom of God. The Apostle John writes in John 1:12, "But as many as received Him, to them He gave the right to become children of God, even to those who believe in His name." Romans 10:13 tells us that "whoever calls upon the name of the LORD shall be saved." Jesus Himself, in John 14:6, said, "I am the way, the truth, and the life. No one comes to the Father except through Me."

God's plan of everlasting life and eternal redemption through His Son Jesus Christ is offered to every man, woman, and child. In Matthew 11:28 Jesus says, "Come to Me, all you who labor and are heavy laden, and I will give you rest." In John 6:37 He says, "All that the Father gives Me will come to Me, and the one who comes to Me I will by no means cast out." In Revelation 3:20 He says, "Behold, I stand at the door and knock. If anyone hears My voice and opens the door, I will come in to him and dine with him, and he with Me." By His unselfish and unconditional love for man, Jesus Christ eliminates all religions, offering in their place a personal relationship with Him.

The Bible assures us in Hebrews 9:27 that "it is appointed for men to die once, but after this the judgment." All sin must be judged. For him who receives Jesus Christ as his personal Lord and Savior, his sins already have been judged on the cross. For those who reject Jesus Christ, eternal judgment is coming. Jesus says in Matthew 10:32-33, "Therefore whoever confesses Me before men, him I will also confess before My Father who is in heaven. But whoever denies Me before men, him I will also deny before My Father who is in heaven."

Peter writes of God's great love for us in 2 Peter 3:9, "The Lord is not slack concerning His promise, as some count slackness, but is longsuffering toward us, not willing that any should perish but that all should come to repentance." The writer of Hebrews 4:7 writes a beautiful plea to all men, "Today, if you will hear His voice, do not harden your hearts."

Won't you accept God's precious invitation now by receiving His Son Jesus Christ as your personal Lord and Savior?

There are four things that you need to do to receive Jesus Christ into your life. In your own words, and from the deepest honesty of your heart:

1. RECOGNIZE, ADMIT and CONFESS that you are a sinner;
2. REPENT, or TURN AWAY, from your sin;
3. BELIEVE that Jesus Christ died on the cross for you and rose from the dead so that you will have everlasting life;
4. INVITE Jesus Christ to come into your heart and life, and to fill you with His Holy Spirit.

If you did those four things and meant them, then, congratulations! You have just become a member of the family of God!

Now, to continue growing and maturing spiritually, there are four simple steps that need to be maintained:

1. PRAY, or talk to God, as much as you can—anytime, anywhere—aloud, or in the quietness of your heart and mind;
2. READ and STUDY the Word of God beginning with the Gospel of John in the New Testament, be sure that you ask God to help you understand what you read, read verse by verse and chapter by chapter, and that you begin memorizing as many Scriptures as you are able;
3. FELLOWSHIP, or gather together, with other

Christians as often as possible to encourage one
another, pray for one another, and praise and worship the Lord;

4. WITNESS, or share your faith in Christ with others, giving out in love what Jesus has given you.

And remember, your relationship with Jesus Christ
develops over a lifetime and into eternity. Your Christian
walk is not a sprint; it is a marathon. Take it one day at a
time and begin each day by focusing your sights on Jesus
only. May God richly bless you and use you for His glory
and honor.

OTHER PRODUCTS FROM
LOGOS MEDIA GROUP

Fury to Freedom (paperback)
The dramatic life story of Raul Ries. To his high school friends he was a dangerous and violent combatant. To his family he was a walking time bomb. To those who fought beside him in Vietnam he was an angry, bitter killer. Only a miracle could save him from destruction. Only a miracle did. *(Available in paperback in English and Spanish.)*

Fury to Freedom (video)
The dramatic life story of Raul Ries as a feature-length film. *(Available on VHS video in English and Spanish.)*

My Husband My Maker (paperback)
Sharon Ries tells of the pain and abuse of living with an angry and violent man, and how, in spite of her own defiance and compromise, God still loved her, restored her, and finally brought her complete fulfillment in life. A story of passionate love and tremendous heartache, crushed hope, utter desperation, and the faithfulness and power of a loving God. *(Available in paperback in English only.)*

A Quiet Hope (video)
Seven Vietnam veterans talk candidly about innocence, war, fear, pain, and guilt. In their own words, tears, and emotions these seasoned veterans bare their souls and scrape open old wounds to offer a complete and total healing to other veterans and their families. Rich with personal accounts, insights, historical footage, and vintage music, this film commentary gives an honest, hard-hitting, and unique perspective to the Vietnam era. Featuring Raul Ries. Running time: 57 minutes. *(Available on VHS video.)*

A Secret Place (video)
The early life story of Ed and Naomi Farrel, missionaries to Colombia, South America, during the war-torn years of the 1940s. Filled with personal accounts, photos, home movies, historical footage, and original music, this documentary is a story of faith, hope, and love played out against the oppositions and hardships of the interior jungles and plains of Colombia. Running time: 67 minutes. *(Available on VHS video.)*

A Venture in Faith (video)
A two-hour documentary on the life of Pastor Chuck Smith and the history and philosophy of the Calvary Chapel movement. A personal look at a man willing to serve God at all costs and the movement of God's Holy Spirit that followed as a result of his obedience. An inside look at a powerful, vibrant, and effective ministry at the close of the 20th Century. Running time: 121 minutes. *(Available on VHS video.)*

The Philosophy of Ministry of Calvary Chapel (booklet)
A concise and simple presentation of the philosophy of ministry that has kept the Calvary Chapel movement a fresh, unique, and Spirit-led segment of the modern church. *(Available in English and Spanish.)*

**For more information on
Logos Media Group products,
or to order, please write:**

**Logos Media Group
22324 Golden Springs Drive
Diamond Bar, CA 91765**